Moreton Morrell Si

SERVICE FAILURE

The Real Reasons Employees Struggle with Customer Service and What You Can Do About It

Jeff Toister

AMACOM

AMERICAN MANAGEMENT ASSOCIATION

New York • Atlanta • Brussels • Chicago • Mexico City • San Francisco
Shanghai • Tokyo • Toronto • Washington, D.C.

Bulk discounts available. For details visit:
www.amacombooks.org/go/specialsales
Or contact special sales:
Phone: 800-250-5308
E-mail: specialsls@amanet.org
View all the AMACOM titles at: www.amacombooks.org

This publication is designed to provide accurate and authoritative information in regard to the subject matter covered. It is sold with the understanding that the publisher is not engaged in rendering legal, accounting, or other professional service. If legal advice or other expert assistance is required, the services of a competent professional person should be sought.

Library of Congress Cataloging-in-Publication Data

Toister, Jeff.
 Service failure : the real reasons employees struggle with customer service and what you can do about it / Jeff Toister.
    p. cm.
 Includes index.
 ISBN 978-0-8144-3199-3 — ISBN 0-8144-3199-2 1. Customer services. 2. Customer relations. 3. Employees—Training of. I. Title.
 HF5415.5.T65 2013
 658.8'12—dc23
                            2012021284

About AMA

American Management Association (www.amanet.org) is a world leader in talent development, advancing the skills of individuals to drive business success. Our mission is to support the goals of individuals and organizations through a complete range of products and services, including classroom and virtual seminars, webcasts, webinars, podcasts, conferences, corporate and government solutions, business books, and research. AMA's approach to improving performance combines experiential learning—learning through doing—with opportunities for ongoing professional growth at every step of one's career journey.

Printing Number

10 9 8 7 6 5 4 3 2 1

CONTENTS

Acknowledgments

I am indebted to many fantastic people who helped make *Service Failure* possible. At the very top of the list is my wife, Sally, whose unwavering support and encouragement continuously inspires me, while her sharp business mind makes her my most trusted colleague.

Many thanks go to a number of people who were instrumental in helping me turn a mountain of research and ideas into a book. Grace Judson, my initial editor, helped me clarify my voice as an author and used her keen eye to make my writing much more readable. My agent, Maryann Karinch, used her experience and wisdom to give me a great sense of optimism about the unknown while giving me a crash course on how to become an author. I also appreciate the kindness and patience of Robert Nirkind, my editor at AMACOM Books, whose guidance helped *Service Failure* become a much better book than it would have been without him.

A special note of appreciation is due to my friend Lori Roth. Her enthusiasm for this project and her amazing professional network were the catalyst that led me to AMACOM Books.

I also appreciate the many customer service professionals who generously shared their experiences with me so I could use their first-hand accounts to provide real challenges and proven solutions to overcoming these obstacles.

Finally, I'd like to thank all of the companies whose employees continuously provide terrible customer service. Without them, I wouldn't have anything to write about.

Introduction

The man walked into a clothing store and spent a few minutes searching for khaki pants, without any luck. He finally spotted an employee and approached him to ask for assistance. "Excuse me," he said. "Do you carry Dockers?"

The sales associate, looking like a deer caught in the headlights, gazed around the immediate area and then stammered, "I don't know."

"You don't know, huh?" the customer responded, walking out of the store without waiting for a reply.

Does this story sound familiar? We all experience poor customer service far too often. Many employees don't seem to care about helping their customers. Even those who do make an effort frequently miss obvious opportunities to provide better service.

It's easy to think of customer service as being a matter of common sense. The sales associate clearly should have known more about the products the store was selling. And if he encountered a question he couldn't answer, he should have found another employee who could provide a knowledgeable response. Instead, he did neither, and the customer walked out the door, the store having lost out on whatever money the customer had intended to spend.

This leads to an important question: Why didn't the sales associate provide better customer service? To learn the answer, you would need to know the employee's version of the story.

It was the sales associate's first day on the job. He was sixteen and had never worked before, so he was nervous. His supervisor had given him a brief tour of the men's department, where he would be working that day, before leaving him alone as she went on her fifteen-minute break. The sales associate had no training, no experience, and hadn't even met his coworkers. He felt totally unprepared and desperately hoped he wouldn't encounter any customers until his supervisor returned from her break and continued his training.

A moment later, the customer approached and asked whether the store carried Dockers.

The sales associate had no idea whether the store carried this product line. He looked around the department in hopes of finding the appropriate section, but had no luck. He also thought about asking someone for help, but he had no idea which of the people milling around the store actually worked there, too. As the customer impatiently stared at him, he unconsciously stammered, "I don't know." The response had been the customer's angry retreat.

You may have guessed by now that the sixteen-year-old sales associate was me. Even I knew what I *should* have done in that moment, but there were stronger forces at play that inhibited my performance. My lack of training made it impossible to answer the customer's question on the spot. Fear and embarrassment robbed me of the confidence I needed to act decisively to find the right answer by either searching the department for Dockers or trying to find a coworker. With no experience to guide me, my instincts weren't sharp enough to prevent me from stammering, "I don't know," when that was exactly what I was thinking. The customer's impatience ensured that I didn't get a second chance.

My story is far from unique. We all know that offering outstanding customer service can mean the difference between growing your business and watching potential sales quite literally walk out your door. Yet many organizations consistently find it a challenge to get employees to serve their customers at the highest level.

There have been plenty of books written about what employees ought to do to provide exceptional service. *Service Failure* examines the real reasons employees struggle to deliver outstanding service, and offers plenty of insights and guidance on overcoming these obstacles, drawing on real stories, scientific research, and my own experiences from more than twenty years as a customer service representative, trainer, manager, and consultant.

Here are just a few things you'll learn:

- How customers are to blame for nearly a third of poor service experiences
- Why your employees might be motivated to deliver bad service
- Why employees may not think customer service is their primary job
- How natural instincts can cause an employee to stop listening to a customer
- What situations can cause employees to give up on serving customers entirely

The benefits of overcoming these challenges are enormous. Companies can develop a reputation for outstanding customer service that translates into better customer retention, increased business through referrals, and improved profitability. Service quality can easily serve as a differentiator in today's highly competitive markets.

Customer service leaders can become more effective at guiding their team's performance. In many cases, you may find the suggestions in this book are counterintuitive or the opposite of commonly accepted wisdom. Knowing what really causes employees to deliver good or bad service is a key insight to apply to developing policies, writing procedures, training employees, or even making hiring decisions that will ultimately lead to better results.

Customer service employees can also gain from learning what motivates their own actions. I still recall how terrible I felt when my first customer left the store on account of my poor service. Examining the reasons why I acted the way I did helped me learn how to do a much better job the next time.

Service Failure is organized into three parts. In Part I, the focus is on *understanding* the obstacles that prevent companies from offering outstanding customer service. We examine why customer service doesn't always come naturally for employees and how this situation can lead to poor service and ultimately hurt a company's bottom line. In Part II, the focus shifts to *overcoming* those obstacles. We identify and explore ten obstacles that stand in the way of outstanding service, reveal insight into why each one is an issue, and share strategies to surmount them. Then, in Part III, we work through practical steps for *implementing these lessons* in your own organization. Throughout the book, you'll find real-life examples from well-known companies, frontline employees, and my own experiences. Common service failures are dissected to understand why they happen and, more important, what can be done to prevent them. Best practices from companies famous for their exceptional service are also analyzed to provide insight into how they've overcome some of these challenges.

One last word of caution as you read on. As you read some of the examples of particularly poor customer service, you may find yourself thinking, "There's no excuse for that behavior!" Of course you'd be right, but keep in mind these stories are nonetheless true. As you'll learn in Chapter 1, even inexplicably rude service may have an explanation after all. And, once you have the explanation, you have the insight necessary to ensure it doesn't continue to happen. Judging by the state of customer service today, that will put you several steps ahead of the competition.

PART I

Understanding Obstacles to Outstanding Customer Service

CHAPTER 1

Customer Service Doesn't Come Naturally

Hidden Obstacles to Serving Customers

The cashier at the fast-food restaurant scowled as I handed him my payment. He looked at the $5 bill I'd given him, glanced at the $4.05 displayed on his register, and then looked back at me asking, "Don't you have a nickel?"

"Sorry," I replied. "All I have is that $5 bill."

The cashier heaved a tremendous sigh, looked me in the eye, and said, "I hate people like you."

I stood in stunned silence while he counted out my change from his cash drawer and slammed the coins on the counter. "There," he said. "Now you have some cents!"

I was speechless and embarrassed. This unprovoked verbal attack was uncalled for in any setting, never mind a customer service situation. Until this moment I never thought any employee needed to have this explained to him.

His boss was standing right behind him, yelling at employees to work faster, so it was clearly pointless to complain. However, the story soon became a favorite in my customer service training classes. Some people accused me of fabricating it since the episode was so outrageous. Others chimed in with their own stories about terrible customer service at the same restaurant.

The situation continued to bother me, even as I told the story again and again. It was such an obvious example of "what not to do" that I couldn't understand the cashier's actions. What would cause a frontline employee to respond so inappropriately in a customer service setting without provocation?

More than ten years later, it finally hit me. Though I still don't believe the cashier was right, I think I now understand what was behind his emotional eruption.

If you've ever been a cashier, you know what a hassle it is when you run out of change. Everything comes to a grinding halt. You stand at your cash register waiting while your manager goes to the safe in the office, retrieves the change, and returns. While the manager is gone you awkwardly stand at the register, not quite knowing what to say while the customer in front of you and the other customers in line are impatiently waiting. When the coins finally arrive you have to break them free of their plastic wrappers and pour them into your cash drawer before you can finally give your customer his change.

Now imagine you run out of change during the lunchtime rush at this fast-food place. The restaurant is crowded with customers. All the registers are open and there's a line at least five deep at each one. The drive-through line snakes around the corner of the building and the parking lot is full. The supervisor is clearly stressed out as he frantically rushes around the kitchen barking orders at employees and putting everyone on edge.

This particular supervisor seems likely to get even more upset if he has to stop whatever he is doing to get change from the office. Meanwhile, there are five impatient, hungry customers in the cashier's line already aggravated by the wait. Waiting a few minutes more while an angry boss fetches change from the safe is only going to make matters worse.

Taking all those circumstances into account, you can imagine that counting out 95 cents might have brought this cashier one step closer to a bad situation he very much wanted to avoid.

I could also tell this cashier didn't like his job. I have trained thousands of frontline customer service employees over the years and often encounter people like him who are angry and frustrated. They tell me how they get paid next to nothing to deal with poor treatment from customers, coworkers, and their boss. And since they perceive that customers are the cause of most of their problems at work, many of them say their customers are the most difficult people to deal with.

This understanding made me wonder about other situations where customer service was inexplicably poor. A mentor once told me that most people inherently want to do a good job. He explained that when people aren't doing their job well, you sometimes have to investigate to find out the root cause of their poor performance. I started to search for hidden obstacles that prevented people from providing outstanding service.

My research revealed one very surprising truth: Humans are not naturally good at customer service! We have the potential to deliver amazing service, and some of us are better at it than others, but every person has significant obstacles to overcome. Difficult bosses, processes and procedures that don't work, and difficult customers can all get in the way. Even our own attitudes and emotions can sometimes make it hard to be great at customer service.

The biggest obstacle of all may be inertia. Many companies, leaders, and employees simply underestimate what it takes to deliver outstanding service. In this chapter we'll look at two of the factors that hold organizations back: the challenge of consistency, and the disconnect between the way companies and customers rate service quality.

The Service Consistency Challenge

Throughout my twenty-plus years in customer service, I've repeatedly heard people refer to customer service as a matter of common sense. This common belief belies the fact that good customer service can be maddeningly difficult to achieve with any consistency.

Companies within the same industry often provide very different levels of service.

Southwest Airlines and United Airlines represent opposite ends of the customer service spectrum. According to the 2011 American Customer Satisfaction Index, Southwest earned an 81 percent customer satisfaction rating, the highest among the major airlines in the United States. United, on the other hand, was tied for second worst, with a 61 percent rating after spending the previous two years in sole possession of last place.[1]

On the surface, it seems easy to understand why these two airlines are so different. Southwest is known for its fun-loving employees, has had books written about its exceptional service, and was even featured in the A&E reality television show *Airline*. United's customer service claim to fame is a music video on YouTube called "United Breaks Guitars" that's been viewed more than 10 million times. The music video, posted by musician Dave Carroll, is a hilarious account of Carroll's repeated attempts to get compensated for a guitar that he claims was broken by United Airlines baggage handlers.[2]

The problem with industry ratings is that they are averages, not absolutes. You're not guaranteed a great experience the next time you fly Southwest, and it's likely that United Airlines will deliver all your luggage unharmed the next time you fly United. Many disgruntled passengers have taken to calling Southwest "Southworst," while United Airlines has a loyal following of dedicated passengers who can't imagine flying with any other carrier. In other words, an *average* rating doesn't necessarily equate to *your* rating.

Stores within the same company may also be miles apart in their dedication to their customers and offer very different levels of service. There are two Best Buy stores within a fifteen-minute drive from my home. The first store is in the city. It's usually crowded, and the sales associates are hard to find when you need them and not very helpful. The second store is in the suburbs. This store does a brisk business, yet the lines are short, there's always someone available to help, and the sales associates are knowledgeable. Unsurprisingly, I go to the second store whenever I can.

I'd give the suburban Best Buy store a five-star customer service rating, but I am only one of thousands of customers. Reviews on Yelp, the user-driven website for rating customer service, only modestly agree with my experience: The city store has a rating of two and a half stars (out of five), while the suburban store has a rating of three stars (the average rating comprises multiple reviews ranging from one to five stars), with some customers vowing never to shop there again because of poor service.[3]

Customer service can even vary widely within the same store or department. There's a diner in my neighborhood that makes a terrific breakfast, serves great coffee, and has warm and friendly waitstaff—all except for one server. For a long time I refused to be seated in her section because her service was so poor. She was unfriendly, inattentive, and frequently made mistakes on my order. Somehow, this person always did a bad job when everyone else was consistently outstanding.

But companies, stores, and individual employees can change as well. United Airlines was once my favorite airline and I dreaded flying Southwest Airlines; now the opposite is true. I've tried the Best Buy store in the city a few times recently and the service seems to have improved. I have even gotten stuck with the bad server at my local diner on a few occasions and have gradually noticed a change in her approach. She became friendlier, more attentive, and started getting all of the orders right. I don't mind being seated in her section anymore and am always impressed that she remembers my usual order.

It's tempting to look at customer service as a matter of common sense, but "common sense" really means "the way I personally see it." There is no one right way to serve every customer. Companies, stores, and individual employees aren't always good or always bad when it comes to service. Customer service is ultimately based on human-to-human relationships, and human beings are infinitely variable.

The service consistency challenge has to be met head-on if you want to deliver outstanding service. That means companies must develop service strategies that meet the needs of a wide range of customers and invest in training for their employees. Customer service leaders need to encourage good performance while accepting that their employees can learn from their occasional mistakes. Employees must develop the flexibility to adapt their approach to each person they serve.

The Customer Service Disconnect

The shipping company DHL ran an advertising campaign throughout 2008 highlighting its commitment to customer service. Television commercials featured various ways that DHL went above and beyond for its customers. Each TV ad closed with an emphatic tagline: "We're putting service back in the shipping business."

DHL's advertising department apparently forgot to check with the rest of the company, because DHL customers didn't agree with this new customer service focus. Customer service ratings continued to be the lowest of the three major package carriers, and in November 2008, DHL announced it was pulling out of the express delivery business in the United States.[4]

The DHL example may seem extreme, but it's not uncommon. A 2006 Bain & Company survey found that 80 percent of companies believed they delivered superior customer service—but the customers of only 8 percent of those companies agreed. The study revealed that many of these companies were so disconnected from their customers' experience that they alienated their most loyal customers by taking actions their management apparently never imagined would cause dissatisfaction.[5] For instance, Chargify, a web-based service that manages billing for small companies, set off a wave of customer dissatisfaction when it suddenly announced a price increase in October 2010. The business had decided to start charging for basic services that up till then had been offered for free, and gave its customers only forty-five days' notice of the pricing model changes. Customers were outraged. They posted angry rants on online technical forums, sent the company harsh e-mails, and vented on Twitter. To them, it was common sense: You don't yank the rug out from under your customers with a sudden price increase.

Chargify's management team saw things differently. From management's perspective, customers using free services were a drain on resources that inhibited the company's growth. They believed the new pricing model would allow them to focus on delivering a higher level of service to their best customers. Cofounder Siamak Taghaddos even tweeted this response to customer criticism: "Moving away from freemium gets rid of freeloaders & bad customers, so you can provide better products & support to the good ones."[6]

Chargify's move may have been driven by sound *financial* strategy, but the execution showed how completely disconnected management was from customers. The company's poor response only made things worse. And that ultimately made it a bad *business* strategy.

Some companies are interested in using customer feedback to gain a better understanding of their customers, but they must still be careful to ensure that the way customer feedback is gathered and presented doesn't create blind spots for organizational leaders. The data can sometimes convince executives that their company is doing well while masking signs of customer dissatisfaction.

Customer service surveys are an example of data that can be misleading. As discussed previously in this chapter, survey scores represent the average of many experiences. These averages can hide pockets of upset customers even if there are enough happy customers to bring up the overall score.

The Gallup Organization published a study in 2006 that examined a telecommunications company with an 88 percent customer satisfaction rating. This rating was the average for the company's entire call center. Things got interesting when Gallup looked at the scores of individual employees. Gallup discovered that customers who dealt with the worst 10 percent of the call center reps had a negative experience nearly 60 percent of the time. These reps were creating more problems than they solved![7]

An executive managing this call center may be tempted to view the 88 percent satisfaction rating as a sign of success. However, relying solely on the aggregate survey results would mask a potentially large problem. The average rating means nothing to the unhappy customer whose phone call is being handled by one of the reps rated in the bottom 10 percent.

Customer complaints are another source of feedback that is easily misunderstood. It's estimated that only 5 percent of upset customers share their feedback directly with a company manager or executive. This makes it tempting for a manager who hasn't received any complaints to assume that customers are generally satisfied.[8]

Managers who do receive complaints don't always recognize them as a sign of a larger problem, either. It's often tempting to write off a complaint as a onetime occurrence, even though many other customers may feel the same way. Some managers even get defensive and attribute criticism to unreasonable customers rather than poor service.

Individual customer service representatives tend to overrate their abilities just as often as companies do. I've run a small experiment many times with many companies, with consistent results. I ask a room full of customer service reps to rate the customer service they personally deliver on a scale of 1 to 5, with 5 being the best. Next, I ask the reps to look around the room and assign a rating to the entire team. On average, the reps rate themselves a 4 while rating the team a 3. The math doesn't add up—which shows that most reps believe they're better than their peers.

Some customer service employees have a difficult time seeing where their own actions fall short, even when it's obvious to everyone else.

The night before I was scheduled to deliver customer service training to employees of an airport parking operation, I decided to do a secret-shopper test at several of the parking lots. My goal was to see how well the cashiers followed the company's basic service procedures, such as greeting customers, smiling, making eye contact, explaining the parking charge, and thanking customers. The results weren't promising: Four out of five cashiers failed to adhere to any of the service standards.

The next day I started the class by introducing myself and explaining the secret-shopper test I had conducted the night before. The cashiers I had shopped were all in the class, but none of them remembered my driving through their lane to pay for my parking. Everyone seemed surprised and even angry that four cashiers had done so poorly.

I didn't share the names of the individual cashiers I had shopped because I didn't want to publicly embarrass anyone. However, many of the participants pressed me to reveal their identities. Among the most vocal participants clamoring for the cashiers' identities to be revealed were the four cashiers who had themselves failed to adhere to the company's basic service procedures! They were so confident in their own abilities that it never occurred to them that they may have been one of the employees who rated poorly on customer service. One of the four cashiers actually stood up and demanded accountability: "Who was it? Who made us look bad?" she asked of her coworkers.

This disconnect reveals that it can be difficult for company leaders and frontline employees to realize they have room for improvement. Corporate managers, removed from their customers by layers of personnel and automated systems, may fail to take action as long as they believe everything is okay. Meanwhile, frontline employees may blame service shortcomings on dumb decisions by management, unreasonable customers, or both, while failing altogether to see where their own efforts do not measure up.

Natural Obstacles to Service Greatness

As mentioned at the start of this chapter, inertia may be the biggest reason companies don't provide better customer service. If you don't think there is a problem, why should you do anything about it? However, employees in organizations that truly want to improve service levels still face significant challenges. Sometimes the solutions to these challenges are right in front of us.

Think back to the cashier at the fast-food restaurant. The cashier's fear of his manager's intimidating style, his dislike for the job itself, and his general disdain for his customers overrode any understanding of what is (and isn't) appropriate to say to a customer who has the temerity to require 95 cents in change. As you'll learn in Chapter 10, emotions tend to overpower logic.

These factors don't excuse the cashier's behavior, which was completely out of line, but they do provide insight into how you can make sure that *your* employees will never say, "I hate people like you!" to any of your customers.

This book examines natural barriers to outstanding service and provides suggestions for navigating over, around, or through them. You'll read some cautionary tales illustrating the dangers of ignoring the unnaturalness of customer service. And you'll learn about companies, departments, and individuals that have overcome these challenges to delivering consistently amazing results.

Notes

1. The American Customer Satisfaction Index, 2011 Airline Industry Results, www.theacsi.org.

2. You can watch Dave Carroll's humorous music video on YouTube: http://youtube/5YGc4zOqozo.

3. These were the ratings for my local Best Buy stores on www.yelp.com in 2011. As is typical, customer service ratings may go up or down over time as more customer reviews are added.

4. Jack Ewing, "DHL to Halt Express Deliveries in U.S.," *Bloomberg Businessweek,* November 10, 2008.

5. James Allen, Frederick F. Reichheld, Barney Hamilton, and Rob Markey, "Closing the Delivery Gap: How to Achieve True Customer-Led Growth," Bain & Company white paper, 2005; available at www.bain.com/bainweb/pdfs/cms/hotTopics/closingdeliverygap.pdf.

6. Jason Del Rey, "Case Study: How to Raise Prices," *Inc. Magazine,* January 20, 2011.

7. John H. Fleming, Curt Coffman, and James K. Harter, "Manage Your Human Sigma," *Harvard Business Review,* July–August 2005, pp. 107–114.

8. John Goodman, "Manage Complaints to Enhance Loyalty," *Quality Progress,* February 2006, pp. 28–34.

PART II

Overcoming Obstacles to Outstanding Customer Service

The Customer Is NOT Always Right

Equipping Employees to Handle Challenging Customers

One of the most challenging obstacles to effective customer service is often the customers themselves. In the world of customer service, horror stories frequently begin with the implicit assumption that the customer was a reasonable, rational, and pleasant person who should have been easy to serve. This is sometimes the case, but the reality is that there are many instances when customers play an active role in creating their disappointing experiences. As the old saying goes, it takes two to tango.

I once sat on a hotel shuttle bus waiting for my ride to the airport while two angry women fumed because the hotel couldn't find their reservation. The bus ran on a route between the airport and two hotels a short distance apart that were run by the same company. The trouble started when the women weren't sure which hotel they were going to and the shuttle driver radioed a coworker for help finding their reservation.

The shuttle now sat in the driveway of one of the hotels while a guest service associate explained to the women that she was doing her best to locate their reservation. The hotel associate was gracious, apologized for the delay, and headed back inside to keep searching. The two women got even more agitated after the associate left, grousing about how stupid she was and swearing they would never stay at the hotel again. The shuttle driver reboarded the bus and attempted to make a little small talk, but the women were so unpleasant that he quickly exited.

The guest service associate came back to the bus a few minutes later. "I apologize for the delay, but we finally figured it out," she said. "We checked with our other hotels in the area after we couldn't find your reservation here. We discovered it had been made at our sister hotel on the other side of town."

The two women sat in stunned silence. All of this hubbub was their fault. The guest service associate gave them the option of staying at the hotel where they currently were, though she cautioned them the rate would be significantly higher. The other option was that the hotel would provide them with a complimentary shuttle ride to the hotel where they had made their reservation.

But the women still weren't happy. They wanted to know why the rates were so much higher at this hotel. The associate calmly explained that rates were a function of a number of factors, including current occupancy levels, the hotel's amenities, and its location. This was a full-service hotel with a beautiful view of the bay; the other property was a limited-service hotel in an industrial part of town. They also wanted to know how far they were from the other property and were upset to learn it would be another twenty-minute bus ride to get there. However, they ultimately decided to accept the shuttle ride and stay at the other hotel.

I was glad to finally be heading to the airport, but the whole situation left me mystified. The problem occurred because the two women made an error. The problem got worse because they expected the hotel to offer them a substantial discount, despite the mistake having been their own. They never even thanked the guest service associate or shuttle driver for being so patient or for offering them a free ride.

In this chapter, we'll reexamine the notion that the customer is always right. You'll see how customers can make mistakes, have unreasonable expectations, engage in self-sabotaging behavior, and even abuse the people they expect to help them. All of these customer behaviors can lead to disappointing service, but there are also solutions that will help your employees overcome these obstacles.

The Customer Is Often Wrong

The phrase "the customer is always right" has become a fixture in our customer service culture, but where did it come from? Some historians attribute it to a quote from Chicago merchant Marshall Field: "Right or wrong, the customer is always right." Others believe the quote actually came from Field's right-hand man, Harry Gordon Selfridge, who went on to open his own successful chain of retail stores. Still others think it's a modification of a quote from the famous hotelier César Ritz: "The customer is never wrong." A few historians attribute it to Philadelphia merchant John Wanamaker.[1]

All four of these men were customer service pioneers in the late-nineteenth and early-twentieth centuries. They introduced customer-friendly policies, insisted on high-quality products and services, and treated their employees much better than most employers at the time. Their versions of "the customer is always right" describe a successful business philosophy rather than a literal rule for doing business.

John Goodman, vice chairman of the noted customer loyalty agency TARP Worldwide, estimates that 20 percent to 30 percent of customer dissatisfaction is a result of the customer making an error or having unrealistic expectations.[2] Unfortunately, many of these customers still believe the customer is literally always right. They assume that any problem is automatically the company's or employee's fault rather than accept their share of the responsibility.

Customers like these can be angry, upset, and unreasonable. I often see airline passengers running late for a flight who loudly complain about the airport's poor layout, the disorganized security checkpoint, and the unhelpful airline employees without acknowledging that their troubles were really caused by arriving at the airport only thirty minutes before their flight. Their anger and frustration causes them to take an intractable position when they lodge their complaint.

Sometimes a customer's mistake can make the difference between evaluating the same experience as outstanding or poor. While scanning Yelp a while ago, I saw that a customer had given my local barbershop a one-star rating. I couldn't believe my barbershop merited such a low rating from anyone, so I read the review.

The reviewer felt the location was convenient and his haircut was good. He even commented on the pleasant shoulder massage the barbers give customers with a vibrating massager at the end of the cut. But the barbershop still received just one star because the reviewer felt the haircut was too expensive at $20. However, the barbershop was not charging $20 for a haircut, but $12.

Perhaps the reviewer would have given a four- or even a five-star rating if he had the correct price in mind. Instead, he wrote a review on Yelp that warned other customers to stay away.

Some customers simply disagree with a company's policies and expect special treatment. While eating breakfast in a café one day, I overheard a customer arguing with his server. He was upset about the café's prices and wanted a discount.

This café, like many restaurants, offers various combination plates, but it also has an à la carte menu. The restaurant entices patrons to order the combination plates with prices that are lower than if the items were ordered à la carte. This patron was upset that he would be charged $6.95 for the eggs, meat, potatoes, and toast special, even though he didn't want the potatoes. The server tried to explain that the meal was still a good deal because the eggs, meat, and toast would cost the customer more if ordered à la carte, but the customer insisted he should receive a discount.

The server called the manager over, and the argument continued. I admired the server and the manager for their patience and tactfulness with this unreasonable guest, but the complaints weren't very pleasant background noise for my breakfast. Finally, after ten minutes of wrangling back and forth, they settled on another selection that the customer felt was fairly priced. The customer scowled as he sat by himself and ate his meal, but he was mercifully silent. When he finished, he paid his bill and walked out without leaving a tip.

Customer service employees often feel stuck when fielding a complaint from a customer who is obviously wrong. Human nature may cause the employee to point out the customer's error, but that's usually an unwinnable argument. A much better solution is to modernize the "customer is always right" philosophy and operate by the rule that the customer should always *feel right.*

The best way to make customers feel right is to help them avoid being wrong, which you do by creating generous, customer-friendly policies.

Zane's Cycles has built a national reputation for outstanding customer service by consistently giving customers more than what seems reasonable. For example, the company's bikes come with a lifetime service guarantee covering all tune-ups and repairs arising from normal use. Zane's Cycles will even give away any part that costs less than a dollar. These generous policies make it more difficult for customers to find anything to be upset about when their bike needs maintenance.[3]

Companies are often afraid to be too generous because they worry about the cost, but Zane's Cycles recognizes the economic advantage of this strategy. Offering a lifetime service program gives customers a reason to come back to the store, where they're likely to buy additional accessories and eventually their next bike. Giving away parts worth less than a dollar cost Zane's Cycles $86 one year, but it also created the opportunity to delight 450 customers.

When a customer does make a mistake, generous policies can empower employees with more options to make a customer feel right.

The two ladies who arrived at the wrong hotel were offered a free shuttle ride even though the hotel was under no obligation to do so. This cost the hotel time and money, but it saved the two women a $20 cab ride and ensured they made it safely to the correct destination. The free shuttle ride helped alleviate their anger and kept the situation from escalating into a confrontation in front of the hotel.

Another important step is to train employees to avoid placing blame and instead refocus on finding a solution. For example, airline passengers who arrive at the airport just thirty minutes before flight time are running late no matter whose fault it is. I've seen passengers' emotions instantly change from anxiety and frustration to gratitude when a compassionate employee escorts them to the head of the ticketing line or to the front of the security checkpoint to ensure they make their flight on time.

A big worry for customer service managers is what to do when a customer's mistake leads to a poor experience and that customer chooses to vent his frustrations in a public forum like Twitter or Yelp. The negative review can be harmful to business, but arguing with the customer online for anyone to see can make the business look even worse. Adopting the "customer should always feel right" philosophy can work here, too.

Best Buy provides a great example of how to tactfully avoid arguments and focus on solutions. Customers often post complaints about products and services in public forums such as Twitter. A dedicated team of the company's customer service professionals monitors these forums and quickly responds to each complaint. The reps acknowledge the customer's frustration and provide their contact information, along with an offer to try to resolve the problem.[4]

This approach works well for three reasons. First, offering to help the customer gives Best Buy an opportunity to rectify a problem. Second, it sends a signal to anyone else who may view the interaction that Best Buy takes customer service seriously. Third, there are many instances where the problem gets resolved and a now-satisfied customer posts a follow-up remark thanking Best Buy for its assistance. In recent years, as the company has endured financial difficulties and suffered a number of well-publicized customer service setbacks, Best Buy's ability to engage some of its angry customers online has been a bright spot that has helped stem a wave of customer defections.

Occasionally, a tired or distracted customer will simply lose the ability to think clearly. This makes it awfully tough for the customer service representative, who has to remember that the customer should always feel right! Once again, the best solution is to avoid arguing with the customer and offer a solution instead. Here's an example from Rama, who worked as a front desk agent at a hotel in Las Vegas:

> I was checking in an older gentleman when he asked me what time it was in Las Vegas. I told him it was 6:05 p.m. He told me that he didn't want the time in Los Angeles, but in Las Vegas. My response was that L.A. and Las Vegas are in the same time zone and it was, indeed, 6:05 p.m.
>
> He informed me that my watch was set to L.A. time because that's where all the hotel employees lived, and I should set it to Las Vegas time, where I commute [to work]. After ten minutes of going around and around with him about the time, I finally realized it was a no-win situation. I looked at my watch, which now said 6:15, and responded, "I am so sorry. You're right; I never adjusted my watch when I got to work today. It's actually 6:18." He accepted that, thanked me, and went up to his room. I knew that the extra three minutes I added in wouldn't make him too early or too late for anything, including his flight home.

Putting employees in the position to say "Yes" instead of "No" helps them avoid confrontations or arguments and allows them to focus on resolving the customer's complaint. When employees are successful at handling these situations, they make their customers feel like they are on the same side. They approach the problem as partners, rather than adversaries, and work with the customer to provide a successful outcome.

Customers Have Varied Expectations

Your customers evaluate the service you provide based on how well you meet their expectations. They believe they have received good service when you have met their expectations, poor service when you have fallen short of their expectations, and outstanding service when you have exceeded their expectations.

The challenge employees face is that all customers have different expectations, and no two customers are exactly the same. Let's consider a hypothetical example where three customers walk into their local grocery store to buy milk, eggs, and bread.

Customer A walks into the store and quickly picks up the milk and eggs. She heads for the bread aisle, where she encounters Jim, a longtime store employee. Jim and customer A exchange hellos as customer A walks by, grabs the bread, and heads for the register. She's in and out in less than ten minutes. All of her expectations have been met, so she'd rate her in-store experience as "Good."

Customer B walks into the store a few minutes later and quickly picks up the milk and eggs. She heads for the bread aisle, where she, too, encounters Jim, the longtime store employee. Customer B pauses and asks Jim which brand of bread is the freshest today. He asks her a few questions and then suggests some freshly baked rolls from the store's bakery department that would be perfect for the sandwiches she plans to make for lunch. He then walks her over to the store's bakery department, where he hands her the warm rolls, which also happen to be on sale. Customer B's expectations have been exceeded by Jim's friendly and helpful service, so she'd rate her experience as "Outstanding."

Customer C walks into the store a few minutes after customer B. She also quickly picks up the milk and eggs and heads for the bread aisle, where she encounters Jim. Customer C is in a hurry, so she doesn't notice Jim smiling and saying "Hello" as she walks by. Unfortunately, customer C is in such a hurry that she drops the carton of eggs as she struggles to reach for a loaf of bread on the top shelf with her hands already full. She angrily mutters that the store doesn't know how to stock bread so that people can easily reach it. She grabs the bread and heads toward the register, leaving the carton of broken eggs in the bread aisle. Customer C leaves the store in a bad mood and without any eggs, so she'd rate her experience as "Poor."

Jim, the store employee, took the same approach with each customer, but there were three different outcomes. His error was assuming that all three customers simply expected him to be friendly and to offer assistance when asked. Customer A may have expected nothing more than a friendly greeting, but Jim wouldn't know that for sure unless he had offered some assistance. Jim lucked out with customer B because she asked him a question that prompted Jim to provide more service. He could have saved customer C from a disappointing experience if he had noticed her struggling to reach the bread and had proactively lent a hand before she dropped the carton of eggs.

Sometimes, two customers can view the same experience very differently. There's a wine bar that I enjoy visiting because it has great service, features local wines, and the bartenders often help me discover something new. I decided to write a review on Yelp after visiting a few times and was surprised by some of the reviews others had written. Many people like me rated the wine bar four or five stars (on a five-point scale), but about a third of the reviews were only one or two stars. When I looked closely I discovered that the comments made by the high and low raters described similar experiences.

These ratings told me that the wine bar offered consistent service, but it wasn't right for everyone. The people who gave it low ratings had expected a more romantic setting with attentive servers. They were surprised by the boisterous atmosphere and disappointed by all the time employees spent chatting with the people at the bar. Ironically, the very things they disliked were cited as positives by the people who gave high ratings.

How can you provide outstanding service if you can't be all things to all people and customers have infinitely variable expectations? The answer lies in how you manage customer expectations and then adapt your service to meet their needs.

The first step is helping customers maintain reasonable expectations. An easy method is to find out if someone is a first-time customer. One of my favorite local restaurants has an unusual menu, so servers are trained to ask customers, "Have you been here before?" If they say "No," the server will take a moment to explain the menu and point out other ways the restaurant is a little unique.

This approach works in other settings, too. Mechanics avoid misunderstandings when they provide a written estimate up front and clearly explain any recommended service. Doctors make their patients feel more at ease when they describe a procedure before conducting an examination. A butcher provides extra confidence when he offers a few grilling tips after helping a customer pick out a few steaks for a backyard cookout.

One caveat when setting expectations is that customers tend to hear what they want to hear. If a customer drops off some clothes at the dry cleaner and is told her clothes will be ready in two to three days, the customer is likely to hear "two days." It's always better to say "three days" if that's the longest it will take. If the clothes are ready in three days, the customer will be satisfied. If they are ready in two days, you have an opportunity to exceed expectations by calling the customer and letting her know her dry cleaning is done early.

The second step in effectively serving a wide variety of customers is to adapt your service to suit customer needs.

I once visited a winery with my wife and parents. The first employee who greeted us was very energetic and outgoing and seemed to know a million jokes and funny lines. Unfortunately, he was more focused on putting on a good show than answering our questions about the wine we were tasting.

This employee eventually became distracted by a large group of people arriving on a tour bus, so a second employee came over to assist us. She was much more reserved but knew a lot about the wines she was pouring. She answered all of our questions and even gave us a sample of a special wine that wasn't on the menu. As she rang up a couple of bottles of the wine we decided to purchase, I couldn't help noticing the first employee's picture on the "Employee of the Month" sign over the cash register. We all agreed the second employee's service was much better.

This experience reminded me of the Platinum Rule of customer service. Many of us have heard of the Golden Rule, which suggests that we treat customers the way we want to be treated. The Platinum Rule is an upgraded version that suggests we treat customers the way *they want to be treated*. This requires employees to listen carefully, ask questions, and adapt their service to each individual customer.

The Self-Sabotaging Customer

Customers are often their own worst enemy when it comes to receiving great service. They inadvertently or sometimes deliberately create obstacles for the employees who are trying to help them. Self-sabotaging customers may not realize they are causing their own frustration (especially if they believe the customer is always right), so they will sometimes get angrier and angrier the more an employee tries to help them.

Some customers struggle to explain what they need, especially when they're in a hurry or angry. Here's an example from Marjorie, a customer service rep for a long-distance telephone company:

> One Sunday afternoon a very angry man called. He started off telling me his 1-800 number wasn't working, and then went off on a string of other issues he had. When I tried to ask him questions about the 1-800 number, he went off on me and told me I was stupid and I obviously didn't know how to do my job. He wouldn't give me any of the information I needed to help him—just told me to figure it out.
>
> I tried repeatedly to tell him that I needed some basic level of information to help him, but he apparently wanted me to be a mind reader. In the end, he said, "I don't care about my 1-800 number, I'm mad

that my calling card doesn't work." The calling card was barely mentioned in his original tirade, but that was the one thing he wanted from the call . . . well, that and to berate a total stranger!

Occasionally, customers will inexplicably and deliberately give misinformation to customer service representatives. Here's an example from Noyan, who worked for an outdoor retailer:

> I had a customer walk up to the counter and tell me that he received a call from us stating the sleeping bag we special-ordered for him had come in. When I asked his name, he replied, "Bill." I hurried back to our stockroom to find his sleeping bag, but after frantically searching for almost five minutes, I couldn't find it. I then checked our call log to see which one of my coworkers contacted him, but his name was nowhere to be found on our list.
>
> I finally realized that no one had ordered Bill's item. When I broke the news to him he was outraged and demanded I find him the item he wanted. "I'm so sorry," I replied, "but we only have one left and it was ordered by Robert, but if he doesn't pick it up by the end of the week it's yours." Suddenly Bill's demeanor completely changed as he calmly replied, "Oh, that's right, I told you guys my name was Robert when I ordered it because I don't like people knowing my real name." After verifying his other contact information, I realized he was telling the truth.

Customer service employees have to deal with a wide range of emotions when trying to serve customers who self-sabotage. It can be frustrating to earnestly attempt to help customers whose actions make it difficult or even impossible to please them. Customer service gets even more difficult when, despite your best efforts to serve, the self-sabotaging customer assumes the problem is your fault.

This frustration can consume an employee's focus, making it hard to see what the employee could have done differently or better. Employees often need a supportive boss or coworker who can help them learn from the situation and come up with a different approach the next time they encounter a similar customer. One of my favorite techniques is a simple exercise called the Circle of Influence.

To do this exercise with an employee, I first draw a circle on a piece of paper. I then explain that everything inside the circle represents what the employee can directly control and everything outside of the circle represents things the employee cannot control. We then revisit the difficult situation and list things the employee can control, such as the way the employee greets the customer. Next, we list things the employee can't control, such as the customer's emotions. Finally, we brainstorm ways the employee can expand his circle of influence to exert greater control over the situation.

I once did the Circle of Influence exercise with a group of social workers who were frustrated by clients who would show up at their office unannounced and then get upset when their social worker wasn't able to see them. One of the simplest solutions identified during this exercise was to proactively call clients to schedule appointments in advance. For the social workers, it took a few extra minutes of their time, but they realized they were spending the same amount of time dealing with angry clients who showed up unannounced.

The Abusive Customer

Think back to the last time you encountered a total stranger who was rude to you. Perhaps an aggressive driver nearly ran you off the road. Or someone at the grocery store kept bumping her cart into the back of your legs while you were waiting in line. Or you might have met your new neighbor when she started screaming at you from across the street because she wrongly assumed you weren't picking up after your dog.

Scenarios like these cause your natural defensive instincts to kick in. Your adrenaline levels increase when you're confronted by an aggressive, angry, and unpredictable person. You naturally focus on trying to get yourself safely out of the situation. Afterward, the memory lingers in a mixture of relief that you're safe and disbelief at the other person's actions.

Now imagine this unpredictable and perhaps angry person is a customer, and it's your job to try to make him happy.

Although not the norm, customers can be abusive. They may yell, scream, rant, rave, and occasionally attack physically as well as emotionally. Dealing with them can be a harrowing experience. Here's an example from Andrew, who has worked as a bartender for more than fifteen years:

> I had ten patrons waiting to get a drink, so I had to move quickly, calmly, and deliver the best I could. I finished with one customer, ran his credit card, and set it down in front of him for him to sign. He was talking to the man next to him, and I finished with that man, setting his credit card down for him to sign. At this point, I was on to the rest of the customers.
>
> One of the two men comes back furious about ten minutes later and blames me for running the wrong credit card. That was not the case; he just thought I did [it wrong]. Apparently he had left with the other man's card instead of his own. The other man was long gone. He begins telling me that I am an idiot and that I need to be fired. He then throws the credit card at my face while demanding that I go out and find the guy who has his credit card.
>
> Needless to say, it worked out in the end. The other guy returned with the credit card later that night and both men got their cards back.

Some customers are so outrageous, their behavior is criminal. Do a Google search on "fast food 911 call" and you'll be treated to story after story of customers calling 911 over customer service disputes. Search "angry McDonald's customer" on YouTube and you can watch an angry, drunken McDonald's customer attacking employees through the drive-through window. Try Googling "unruly airline passenger" and you'll read stories of angry passengers disrupting flights; some of their behavior is so bad that it has prompted concerns about terrorist activity.

Customer service can be tough enough as it is, but abusive customers can make service virtually impossible. The solution to working with these select few customers is simple: Invite them to take their business elsewhere. These customers often represent a net loss for your business after you subtract the cost of discounts, service recovery, and extra employee time from the revenue they bring in. Many of them create an unpleasant scene that negatively impacts other customers and drives them away, too. Perhaps most important, these customers subject your employees to hostile, intimidating, or abusive behavior that can create an environment where your employees don't want to work.

Customer service leaders should expect a lot from their employees, but they should demonstrate a strong commitment to them in return. When I was a customer service manager, I could tell how grateful my employees were when I calmly and professionally explained to customers that they couldn't yell and curse at our employees. Sometimes, these customers changed their demeanor after speaking with a manager, and other times they simply decided to take their business elsewhere. No matter what the result, I always saw my employees renew their commitment to customer service because they knew I supported them.

Solution Summary: Overcoming Challenging Customers

Understanding the role that customers play in their service experience isn't an excuse for poor employee performance. As you'll see in subsequent chapters, poor customer service can often be attributed to poor employee performance, poor leadership, poor policies and procedures, or all of the above.

However, customer service leaders must understand *all* the reasons it can be so challenging to make customers happy—including the fact that the customer *isn't* always right.

Here is a short summary of the solutions presented in this chapter:

- Create generous, customer-friendly policies that make it easier for customers to be right.
- Train employees to avoid placing blame when a customer makes an error, and to focus on finding a solution instead.

- Avoid arguing with customers in public forums such as Twitter, but publicly acknowledge their feelings and offer to address the issue in private.

- Identify new customers and take a moment to let them know what they can expect so that they won't encounter any unpleasant surprises.

- Remember that customers tend to hear what they want to hear, so be careful not to be overly optimistic when setting expectations.

- Operate by the Platinum Rule: Treat customers the way *they* want to be treated.

- Learn how to get better results with self-sabotaging customers by conducting a Circle of Influence exercise.

- Invite abusive customers to take their business somewhere else to prevent them from draining resources, driving away other customers, and discouraging employees.

Notes

1. The Phrase Finder gives a nice overview of the history of "The customer is always right" at www.phrases.org.uk/meanings/106700.html. John Wanamaker is credited as the author of this saying on a website for Macy's in the Wanamaker Building in Philadelphia; see www.visitmacysphiladelphia.com/groups.cfm.

2. John Goodman shared this statistic in his presentation called "Treating Employees as Customers," the International Customer Management Institute (ICMI) Dreamforce 2010 conference, San Francisco, December 8, 2010.

3. Chris Zane, *Reinventing the Wheel: The Science of Creating Lifetime Customers* (Dallas: BenBella Books, 2011).

4. You can view Best Buy's discussions with customers on its Twitter feed: @twelpforce.

$$\textcircled{F}$$

CHAPTER 3

They're Your Customers, Not Mine

Aligning Employees' Interests with Those of the Company

The phone message wasn't good news. The caller was reminding me that my new grill would be delivered that morning. The problem was I'd scheduled an afternoon delivery. My wife had even arranged to leave work early so that she could be home when the grill arrived, but nobody would be there if they came in the morning.

I called back to see if the delivery schedule could be corrected and got an employee named Chris on the phone. I calmly explained that the grill was scheduled to be delivered that afternoon, not that morning.

"Who told you that?"

Ah, four of the worst words a service rep can say to an irritated customer. Chris had an opportunity to fix the problem, but instead he focused on laying the blame somewhere else. He accused the store associate who had sold the grill of getting the delivery schedule wrong. Chris tried to further distance himself from the error by explaining that deliveries were handled by a separate department that only made deliveries where and when it was told to by the store.

None of this information mattered to me, and I didn't care whose fault it was. My goal was getting my grill delivered in time for a cookout I had planned that weekend, and sparing my wife the hassle of needlessly taking time off from work. Chris was unable or unwilling to honor the original delivery schedule, so it ultimately took quite a bit of back-and-forth to reschedule the delivery for another date when I knew I would be home all day.

Customer service problems often occur because an employee fails to take ownership of a situation. In this chapter, we'll explore the reasons employees don't necessarily share their employers' customer service goals. We'll also examine how efforts to direct employee behavior, such as offering financial incentives, employee recognition, or establishing customer service standards, often have unintended consequences. Customer service leaders need to know how to avoid these pitfalls if they want to motivate their employees to serve customers at the highest level.

The Principal-Agent Problem

Customers usually view employees as representatives of the entire company, but employees often see themselves as individuals who are separate from their employer.

I was frustrated with my experience getting my new grill delivered, and Chris was a part of that poor experience. It didn't matter to me that someone in one department sold the grill and someone in another department delivered it. As far as I was concerned, they were all employees of the same company. The salesperson who sold me the grill had agreed on a delivery date and time, and I expected Chris to honor that agreement.

Chris obviously saw things differently. His insistence on identifying a culprit for the scheduling mishap indicated that he wasn't consciously responding as a representative of his company. He was acting as an individual whose day just got more challenging because another employee didn't properly schedule a product delivery.

Economists refer to the relationship between companies and their employees as the "principal-agent problem." A company (the "principal") hires employees (the "agents") to perform work on behalf of the company. The employees will ideally represent their employer's best interests, but of course they're also people who have their own motivations.

The principal-agent, or employer-employee, relationship has two primary challenges: First, the goals of the employer and employee can come into conflict. Second, employees operate with a certain degree of autonomy since the employer can't monitor and control all of their actions. This autonomy can make it tempting for employees to pursue their own self-interest, even if it comes at the expense of their employer.[1]

Both these challenges were evident during my conversation with Chris. It was in the company's best interest for him to take ownership of the problem and make sure my grill got delivered so the company could keep me as a happy customer. Yet Chris seemed motivated by a desire to avoid blame. He was acting autonomously by attempting to disassociate himself from the problem and the other department, rather than acting on behalf of his employer and providing a solution.

It's not difficult to find other examples where employees autonomously pursue their own goals instead of their employer's. An employee who takes a cigarette break in front of the store's entrance may look unsightly to customers, but it saves her from having to spend half of her break time walking to and from the designated smoking area behind the store. A retail sales associate may carry on a conversation with a coworker to avoid helping people. A delivery driver may drive like a maniac in the company van, weaving in and out of traffic to get to his destination more quickly, even though he is creating an obvious safety hazard in a vehicle marked with the company logo.

I once went into a gift shop and discovered the item I wanted was sold out. When I asked a salesperson to call a sister store to see if it had what I was looking for, he dialed the number and then handed the phone to me, saying, "Here, you talk to her. I can't stand that lady!" You would never expect someone to act that way until you realize that his goal, which was to avoid talking to a coworker he disliked, was more important than his company's goal to provide customers like me with assistance. The salesperson was also acting autonomously because there wasn't anyone else working in the store to observe or correct his behavior.

This situation reveals another complication in the employer-employee relationship: Employees control information regarding their interactions with customers, which means it's unlikely the supervisor will become aware of an employee providing poor service if the supervisor doesn't observe it directly. Many customers never complain about poor service from employees, and when they do, those complaints often fail to reach a supervisor.

John Goodman estimates that 90 percent of customer complaints are directed to frontline employees.[2] If employees aren't at fault, you might expect them to take action to resolve the problem or pass the complaint along to someone who can address the issue. But what if handling the complaint isn't in an employee's best interests?

There are several explanations for why an employee might not want to address a customer complaint or pass it along to management:

- The employee fears being reprimanded for causing the complaint.
- The employee thinks the complaint will not be properly addressed by management, so sharing the information is a waste of time.
- The employee views handling the problem as an annoyance or inconvenience.
- The employee believes he was treated poorly by the customer, so intentionally mishandling the complaint is a means to exact revenge.

To overcome the principal-agent problem, employers need to find a way to align their interests with their employees' personal motivations. This begins with the hiring process. It's not enough to simply hire someone with the right skills to do the job. Companies must hire employees who will love the job and love your company.

The starting point is to make a list of the essential traits or characteristics an employee must have to enjoy working for your company. If you offer a high-energy, fast-paced work environment, then you'll need employees who love that type of work. Someone who prefers a slow and deliberate work style would probably not be a good fit.

The next step is to test the employee's fit through screening, interviewing, and training. Online retailer Zappos is known for having committed, customer-friendly employees. Part of this commitment comes from an unusual offer made to all new hires after their first week of training. New employees are told they can receive $2,000, in addition to what they've already earned, if they choose to resign before the end of their four-week training program. While fewer than one percent of employees accept the offer, it's a true test of whether employees feel they belong.[3] Employees will also remember that they turned down $2,000 to stay with the company.

Another way to align employee interests with company goals is to involve employees in decision making. Soliciting employee input on designing work procedures, creating customer service strategies, and setting goals helps them gain a sense of ownership. When employees are asked to help write a new policy, they are more likely to understand its importance and meaning.

Involving employees can also convince them to agree to tasks they might otherwise find objectionable. When I worked for a catalog company, our call center representatives were expected to pitch a store credit card offer to certain preapproved customers. Unfortunately, most of our reps had a negative impression of the credit card and were uncomfortable offering it to customers. As a result, there was a meager 5 percent acceptance rate.

As the call center's training supervisor, I was instructed to devise a training program that would improve our sales performance. The first thing I did was identify a few employees who were highly successful. Some of them got as many as 40 percent of their customers to accept the credit card by enthusiastically promoting several of its features and benefits. It was easy to build a simple training program around the successful formula used by these reps.

When I rolled out the training I was able to get buy-in from participants by explaining that the techniques they were learning came from their coworkers. I also shared the features and benefits that these employees found got the most positive reactions from customers. Even the most skeptical employees were willing to give the new approach a try once they knew people like them had used it. After training thousands of employees over a few months, we were able to increase our average acceptance rate to 20 percent and observed many more reps enthusiastically offering the credit card to their customers.

The final piece of the puzzle is an ongoing dialogue between frontline employees and their supervisor. Employees are more likely to develop bad habits or deliver poor service if they aren't properly monitored. Supervisors should regularly observe employee performance and offer praise for good results while providing constructive feedback when employees stray from the guidelines. This continual feedback keeps employees aligned with company goals and prevents them from going too far astray.

This level of involvement can be challenging for supervisors who find it hard to make time to supervise their employees. They may be overwhelmed with administrative duties, have employees working on several shifts or in different locations, or simply have too many direct reports to pay careful attention to each one. In the big picture, companies must carefully design their supervisors' responsibilities so that they have the ability to spend time coaching and developing their employees. At an individual level, supervisors who work hard to encourage good performance soon discover they have to spend much less time correcting mistakes.

Some supervisors find it easy to spot negative performance, but they have a difficult time remembering to recognize and praise an employee for doing something well. One solution that they may find helpful is to create a simple system to help remind them to spot and encourage positive performance. I know a supervisor who would start each day with five coins in his right pocket. Each time he commended an employee for doing something well he'd take one of the coins and put it in his left pocket. His goal each day was to move all the coins from the right to the left pocket so that he knew he'd made at least five positive observations.

Customer service levels can improve dramatically when employees and employers share the same interests. Employees are much more likely to follow procedures, adhere to policies, and give extra effort when they are committed to the company's goals. They are also more likely to share rather than suppress valuable customer feedback that can be used for continued improvement.

The Problem with Financial Incentives

Companies often try to solve the principal-agent problem by providing financial incentives for good performance. The assumption is that employees are more likely to act in their employer's best interests if there's money on the line. Unfortunately, financial incentives often cause unintended consequences that can lead to worse rather than better service.

Sales commissions are a common form of financial incentive, but they can lead to all sorts of negative results. They may encourage unethical conduct, reduce cooperation among employees, and cause salespeople to focus so much on earning commissions that they ignore other customer service issues. In some extreme cases, sales commissions may lead to fraud or other illegal behavior.[4]

One of the most famous cases occurred in 1992 when Sears, Roebuck & Company was investigated by several state consumer affairs agencies for alleged fraud and deceptive practices in its automotive department. These investigations found that auto mechanics who earned commissions on the revenue they generated consistently recommended unnecessary repairs in an effort to meet sales goals and earn more money. Sears ultimately eliminated sales commissions for its auto mechanics as a result.[5]

Employees who receive tips can help us understand the impact of financial incentives for customer service as well. Many service workers, such as food servers, valet parking attendants, and taxi drivers, depend on tips for a substantial part of their income. However, customer service is only one of several factors that influence the size of a tip. Michael Lynn, a professor at Cornell University's School of Hotel Administration, has conducted extensive research on restaurant tipping and concludes that service quality influences tipping amounts by an average of only 2 percent.[6]

Social norms and customs provide guidelines for tipping that are generally followed unless customers receive what they perceive as exceptionally poor or exceptionally good service. Furthermore, since tipping is usually based on a percentage of the bill, a customer who orders a bottle of wine in a restaurant will almost certainly tip more than a customer who orders a soda yet receives the same level of service. There are also individual customers who are particularly cheap or incredibly generous when it comes to tipping, so their unusually small or large tips won't be an accurate reflection of their server's performance.

Like sales commissions, tipping can result in unintended consequences. Some servers may withhold service from customers they believe will tip poorly. Teamwork may suffer among tipped employees if they believe the extra effort to cooperate won't result in additional income, and employees might avoid tasks that don't directly result in a tip.

In a perfect world, employees would be intrinsically motivated to do their job at a high level without any financial incentives. But sales commissions and tips can be an important part of an employee's income, so it isn't always practical to completely eliminate them. Businesses that believe they must offer these incentives should carefully design and monitor their use to ensure employees don't have a strong incentive to treat customers poorly.

One best practice is to align financial incentives with team goals rather than individual ones. Notable entrepreneur and *Inc. Magazine* columnist Norm Brodsky puts his salespeople on the same bonus system as the rest of his employees rather than a sales-based commission. The result has been a stable sales force that consistently outperforms the competition by working closely as a team and emphasizing long-term customer relationships.[7]

Tipped employees should pool their tips rather than keep everything they individually collect. While this practice may discourage a few of the highest earners, it promotes more teamwork. When I worked for a parking company, valet locations that pooled their tips had consistently higher service levels than locations that did not. One of our locations switched to a tip pooling system and immediately saw valets take a greater interest in activities that impacted service but didn't directly lead to tips, such as greeting arriving vehicles and helping guests unload their luggage.

You see the same effect in restaurants. When tips are shared, servers are more likely to help guests in someone else's section. This team approach raises overall service levels and ultimately increases the tip pool.

Customer service leaders must also monitor employees who receive financial incentives just as closely as they would other employees. Supervisors should never assume that a commission, tip, or bonus provides enough motivation for employees to consistently provide great service. All service employees need periodic coaching and feedback, regardless of how they are paid.

The Unexpected Side of Employee Recognition

Some customer service leaders use recognition programs in lieu of financial incentives as a way of encouraging employees to act in their company's best interests. They offer small rewards for achieving goals. Unfortunately, even employee recognition programs can backfire.

Steve was the parking operations manager for a large sports stadium. One day, he bought doughnuts for his employees as a way to recognize their hard work and great customer service. The doughnuts were such a hit that he bought them again before the next game. This soon became a tradition, and Steve brought in dozens of doughnuts every time there was an event.

Steve's employees were initially delighted by the treats, but they soon learned to expect them every time. Some employees got discouraged if they didn't get their favorite variety, while others got upset with coworkers who made off with more than their fair share. A few employees even complained about getting only doughnuts but never bagels or other pastries.

Steve soon discovered that a reward's motivational value quickly diminishes once it becomes expected. He realized the doughnuts were no longer considered recognition, yet his employees would be disappointed if he didn't bring them. He summed up the lesson nicely by saying, "Be careful what you start."

Some managers use games, contests, and prizes to promote internal competition and to motivate employees to give extra effort. These motivators also have a hidden trap that can lead to unintended consequences. Employees can easily focus too much of their attention on winning the prize while losing sight of the big picture. I remember one such contest when I worked at a clothing store as a teenager.

Christie, the store manager, announced one day that the person who helped the most customers over the course of a week could write his own work schedule for the following week. From my perspective, that was a huge prize, so I went out of my way to help every customer I could and ended up the winner. Christie ran the contest the next week, and I won again, aided in part by my plum work schedule. She finally discontinued the contest when she realized having one part-time employee (me!) name his own hours created scheduling challenges for all the other employees.

The contest may have been great for me, but it hurt both customer service and sales because it gave me an incentive to concentrate on behaviors that would help me win. Since the contest was based on the number of customers assisted rather than on sales, I tried to interact with as many customers as possible. This meant limiting the amount of time I spent with any one person so that I could move on to the next one. It also took my attention away from other duties, such as keeping the dressing rooms clean, refolding clothes in my department, and checking stock for people who called the store.

Recognition can be used as an effective employee motivation tool, but it must be unexpected and occur after a desired outcome is achieved. This way, recognition becomes a way of showing appreciation for good work rather than a means of incentivizing behavior.[8] That's why Steve's doughnuts were so well received the first time but were soon taken for granted when they became part of the routine.

Unexpected rewards also eliminate the possibility of employees changing their behavior just to win a prize. A client of mine worked diligently to improve its customer service survey scores and encouraged every employee to work toward the team goal. It was only after the employees achieved their objective that my client threw a big party to celebrate their accomplishment. Had the company announced the party ahead of time, the employees' performance might have declined afterward since the celebration would feel like the end of a journey. The party made employees feel appreciated for what they had accomplished, and making it a surprise motivated them to continue to improve their performance.

Customer Service Standards That Backfire

The industrial era led to the development of management methods that emphasize strict adherence to standard operating procedures. This approach works well in a manufacturing environment where the goal is to produce each widget quickly and to exactly the same specifications. But a series of well-defined processes tends to fall short when applied to relationships between human beings.[9]

My local grocery store has a policy that requires checkers and baggers to ask customers if they'd like assistance carrying their purchases to the car. The standard was put into place to foster a consistent level of service and to make sure customers didn't feel discriminated against when one customer was offered assistance while another wasn't. Unfortunately, this requirement leaves no room for employees to use their own discretion. I once purchased a single pack of gum and my cashier dutifully asked, "Do you need any help out to your car today?"

Service standards like these place employees' attention on a task (offering assistance) rather than an outcome (customer satisfaction). Employees know they may be monitored by their supervisor or even a secret shopper with a checklist of required actions. Failure to fulfill all the required actions could lead to disciplinary action. On the other hand, employees might receive a small bonus or another form of recognition for maintaining 100 percent compliance with the required customer service actions.

This creates the potential for an employee to receive praise for complying with internal service standards while delivering poor service in the eyes of the customer. Being asked if I needed assistance carrying my pack of gum to the car felt awkward and inauthentic. At the same time, the employee did exactly what she was supposed to do.

Call centers are notorious for requiring their customer service reps to adhere to a long list of standard responses. These calls really are monitored for "quality assurance and training purposes" by a supervisor or quality assurance technician who listens to the call and verifies whether each requirement is met. Unfortunately, these requirements often have little to do with customer satisfaction. Reps who answer the phone using the correct scripted greeting might get points for compliance even if they deliver the greeting in a monotone voice completely devoid of warmth and enthusiasm. On the other hand, reps may be disciplined for failing to upsell even if the customer specifically says, "I don't want to buy anything else or hear about any other products today."

Some customer service standards may sound terrific in a marketing meeting but fail to resonate when put into practice. I was once out shopping for shoes and, right after making my selection, stepped into a short line to wait for a cashier. When it was my turn, the cashier called me over by saying, "I can help the next shoe lover over here." That phrase may have been engineered to accurately reflect the shoe store's brand positioning strategy, but it felt forced and a little weird in practice.

Like financial incentives and recognition, customer service standards can sometimes lead to unintended negative consequences. A company that provided computer support for its clients routinely included a service-level agreement (SLA) in its contracts. The SLA stipulated an average response time for handling trouble tickets submitted by the client. The service provider's employees quickly found a loophole in the agreement and began closing trouble tickets without verifying that the problem had been corrected. In many cases, the problem hadn't been fixed, so the client had to open a new trouble ticket since the previous one was closed. This created an additional hassle for the client, but the practice helped employees meet the standard for average time to close a ticket.

Companies are right to try to create a consistent customer experience, but they'll find that broad guidelines rather than rigid standards often work best. Guidelines allow employees to adapt to each individual customer's needs. Ironically, most employees are more likely to act in their employer's best interests when a checklist of standards is replaced by clear goals.

Nordstrom consistently ranks at the top of a number of customer service surveys, including the American Customer Satisfaction Index. Nordstrom is perhaps the best-known example of a company using broad goals rather than task-based standards to guide employee behavior. All Nordstrom employees receive a five-inch by eight-inch index card that states that the number-one goal is outstanding customer service. The card goes on to explain that the one and only rule is to "use good judgment at all times."[10]

Broad guidelines also allow employees to use their individual personalities to make the service they provide more authentic. True Value is consistently recognized for its hardware stores that offer outstanding customer service. Part of True Value's success comes from a policy of encouraging each employee to rely on his own unique personality. My local True Value hardware store requires employees to greet customers immediately and offer them assistance. How they do it is up to them, as long as it makes customers feel welcome and results in customers finding what they came in to buy.

An employee once greeted me by saying, "What are *you* doing in here?" I had already made several unexpected trips to the store because I was doing a home project, and this employee had helped me several times over the span of a few days. Each time, we joked that we hoped this would be the last time I'd have to come back in to get supplies for this particular project. This greeting was his friendly way of telling me that he hoped I would soon succeed in completing my project. It put a smile on my face and made me feel quite welcome.

Solution Summary: Getting Employee Buy-in

Aligning employees' motivation with their company's interests can be a challenging task, but it's an essential part of building an organization capable of delivering outstanding customer service. Companies should strive to put employees in a position where their intrinsic motivation leads them to the right action, rather than try to manipulate employees through incentives that may have negative side effects.

Here is a summary of the solutions presented in this chapter:

- Hire people who will love their job and love your company, so they'll naturally want to do what you ask them to do.
- Involve frontline employees in decision making and problem solving so that they will take ownership of company goals.

- Frequently monitor employee performance so that you can recognize positive achievements and correct mistakes.

- If you must use financial incentives such as commissions or tips, be sure to align them with team goals rather than individual accomplishments.

- Don't assume that commissioned or tipped employees need less supervision than employees who aren't paid by their performance. They require the same monitoring and coaching as anyone.

- Make employee recognition an unexpected event and offer it only after good performance. This approach shows employees they are appreciated while keeping their focus on customer service rather than earning a prize. Use broad service guidelines rather than detailed standards to allow for more flexibility and personalization.

Notes

1. Kathleen M. Eisenhardt, "Agency Theory: An Assessment and Review," *Academy of Management Review* 14, no. 1 (1989), pp. 57–74.

2. John Goodman shared this statistic in his presentation called "Treating Employees as Customers" at the International Customer Management Institute (ICMI) Dreamforce 2010 conference, San Francisco, December 8, 2010.

3. Tony Hsieh, *Delivering Happiness: A Path to Profits, Passion, and Purpose* (New York: Hachette Book Group, 2010).

4. Lisa D. Ordóñez, Maurice E. Schweitzer, Adam D. Galinsky, and Max H. Bazerman, "Goals Gone Wild: The Systematic Side Effects of Over-Prescribing Goal Setting" (working paper, Harvard Business School, Cambridge, 2009).

5. Lawrence M. Fisher, "Sears Auto Centers Halt Commissions After Flap," *New York Times*, June 23, 1992.

6. Robert J. Kwortnik Jr., W. Michael Lynn, and William T. Ross Jr., "Buyer Monitoring: A Means to Insure Personalized Service," *Journal of Marketing Research* 46, no. 5 (October 2009), pp. 573–583.

7. Norm Brodsky and Bo Burlingham, *The Knack: How Street-Smart Entrepreneurs Learn to Handle Whatever Comes Up* (New York: Penguin Group, 2008).

8. Daniel Pink, *Drive: The Surprising Truth About What Motivates Us* (New York: Riverhead Books, 2009).

9. John H. Fleming and Jim Asplund, *Human Sigma: Managing the Employee-Customer Encounter* (New York: Gallup Press, 2007).

10. Patrick D. McCarthy and Robert Spector, *The Nordstrom Way: The Inside Story of America's #1 Customer Service Company* (New York: John Wiley & Sons, 1995).

CHAPTER 4

Your Employees Are Double Agents

*Bridging the Gap Between Doing the Right Thing for the
Customer and Following Company Policy*

Some customer service situations are frustrating for both the customer and the employee. I had one of these mutually challenging experiences when I purchased a paper shredder at my local office supply store. The shredder was intended to replace one I'd thought was broken, but after returning home with the new shredder I discovered that the old shredder had stopped working because of a user error. (It appears those safety features designed to protect you from shredding your fingers actually do work!) This seemed like a happy discovery until I looked at the receipt and saw it was clearly marked Exchanges only—no returns.

This "no shredder returns" policy was apparently an exception to the store's 100 percent satisfaction guarantee that allows you to return an item for a refund within thirty days of purchase. I hadn't removed the new shredder from the box, so I took it back to the store and tried to return it, despite the warning on the receipt. The customer service associate listened to my story and then meekly explained that shredders could not be returned.

"Can I get store credit?" I asked. The associate told me they weren't able to provide store credit, even though the shredder hadn't been removed from the box.

I tried another tactic. "I know this was my mistake, but are there any other options besides being stuck with a shredder I don't want or need?"

This was a no-win situation for the employee. He obviously saw the logic of my argument, but he was under strict instructions not to allow any shredders to be returned. He could violate the store's policy and return the shredder, but then he'd likely get in trouble. He could refuse to return the shredder, but then he'd run the risk of making a customer angry who would probably complain to his boss.

The employee finally offered to get his manager to see what he could do.

I retold my story when the store manager appeared, acknowledged my error, and asked him for his assistance. The manager looked at my unopened shredder and quickly realized the "no shredder returns" rule wasn't written for my situation. To my surprise and pleasure, he promptly refunded my money.

In this chapter, we'll see how service failures like the one I narrowly avoided can occur when employees are forced to balance the competing needs of their employer and their customers. We'll examine how customer service representatives ultimately make decisions that are in their own best interests when these types of conflicts occur. We'll even look at some surprising research that suggests customer service leaders are more likely to create these sorts of situations when they don't have direct customer contact.

The Double Agent Problem

In Chapter 3, we examined the principal-agent problem, where companies sometimes struggle to get their employees to act on their behalf. Customer service employees can often feel like double agents because they serve two principals: their employer and the customer. As a result, three sets of self-interest are present, and potentially competing, in every customer service interaction.[1]

Let's look at the office supply store example and imagine each party's interests in this situation (as summarized in Figure 4-1).

Figure 4-1. One customer service interaction, three sets of self-interest.

Party	Interests
Store Manager	Sell paper shredders at a reasonable profit. Used shredders cannot be reconditioned and sold as new, so accepting returns hurts profitability.
Store Employee	Do the best job possible. This includes not getting in trouble with the manager or making customers angry.
Me	Return the shredder for a refund or store credit. I don't want to get stuck with an expensive shredder I don't need.

Are the three parties' interests incompatible? The store manager's "no returns or exchanges" policy certainly makes it seem that way to the employee. The policy was written because the store can't resell a shredder that's been used, and management wanted to provide employees and customers with clear and unambiguous guidance. But my situation was a gray area that couldn't easily be addressed with a black-and-white policy. The shredder hadn't been removed from the box and could be resold even though the employee didn't have the authority to make the right decision. He was stuck between the policy and common sense.

Rigid policies that don't allow for employee discretion, even when they become absurd or unfriendly to customers, can lead to a double agent problem. A stadium concession stand may be covering its legal risk by requiring employees to check ID on anyone buying alcohol, but it could be annoying to a seventy-year-old customer with gray hair and a wrinkled face who didn't bring his ID when he went to buy a beer. A customer who calls her cable company to discuss a billing issue may not be in the mood to hear the customer service rep make a required sales pitch about premium channels. A store that requires customers to check their bags at the front may deter a few thieves but may also turn off quite a few customers who are made to feel that they can't be trusted not to steal.

Employees who feel caught in the middle can sometimes make matters even worse if they try to remain neutral. Some double agents have even developed their own customer service phrases that highlight their frustration. If you've ever encountered a double agent you may have heard a few of these phrases:

"Hey, I don't make the rules."

"I just do what I'm told to do."

"You'll have to ask the boss why we do it this way."

Do any of those phrases sound familiar? They are used by employees attempting to disassociate themselves from their company. But, as you may recall from Chapter 3, customers tend to view the company and the customer service representative as one and the same. Double agent employees who try to remain neutral may come across to customers as just lazy or uncaring; rather than engendering any sympathy for their dilemma, their comments and behavior have the opposite effect.

Companies offering outstanding customer service avoid creating double agents by eliminating the potential for conflict between their customers and their employees—and that means eliminating the factors that create double agents in the first place. They rigorously avoid policies that are obviously unfriendly to their customers. They try to see beyond the value of each individual transaction to understand the value of a happy customer, and they empower their employees to do the same.

Companies set rigid policies because they worry about customer abuse or employee error. For example, the office supply store may worry about losing money if it allowed customers to return shredders that couldn't be resold. Giving employees the discretion to determine if merchandise is resalable may not ameliorate such a problem in the minds of corporate policy makers if they don't trust their frontline employees to make good decisions.

You have to speak the language of business to get past this fear, so let's see what happens when we run some numbers on shredder returns. The average gross margin for retail office supplies is 38.7 percent.[2] That means a $100 shredder costs the store an estimated $61.30 ($100 − [38.7 percent × 100]). By this estimate, the store stands to lose $61.30 if it accepts a returned shredder that can't be resold or returned to the manufacturer. That looks like a sizable loss on one item.

Now let's look at the bigger picture. I spend an average of $500 per year at this store. This translates to an annual gross profit of $193.50 at a 38.7 percent average gross margin. When we compare that to the potential loss of $61.30 on the shredder return, we see that my average contribution to the office supply store's profitability is more than three times what the store would lose by refunding my money for a shredder that can't be resold.

The business case now looks a little different. The store could lose $61.30 if it took back a shredder that can't be resold, but it would lose $193.50 that year if it refused the return and I decided to take my business to a competitor. Of course, the store wasn't in danger of losing anything since the shredder I returned was unopened and could easily have been resold. In retrospect, the frontline customer service associate was needlessly put in a double agent position by a bad policy.

L.L.Bean is an example of a company that has built a reputation for outstanding customer service with the help of a generous returns policy.

The retailer realizes the key to long-term success is making sure customers are happy with their products and trusting that the majority of customers won't abuse this generosity. This philosophy helped L.L.Bean earn the number-one ranking on *Businessweek*'s 2010 Customer Service Champs list.[3] The company's return policy is clearly posted on its website. Here is what is says:

> Our products are guaranteed to give 100% satisfaction in every way. Return anything purchased from us at any time if it proves otherwise. We do not want you to have anything from L.L.Bean that is not completely satisfactory.[4]

L.L.Bean's return policy means its employees aren't stuck between the customer and the company when a customer is unhappy with a purchase. According to a former L.L.Bean employee named Dennis, customer service representatives are instructed to make it easy for a customer to return a purchase: "It was never a question about returns. Customers would call to ask how to return something, and I'd just give them the information on how to return it."

Creating policies that some customers won't like can sometimes be unavoidable. A coffee shop may impose a one-hour time limit on customers sitting at a table during peak hours because without the policy people would take up tables for half the day at the expense of other customers. However, frontline employees should still be given as much discretion as possible when it comes to enforcing this policy. A one-hour time limit may make sense when people are waiting for a place to sit, but it would seem unfriendly on a slow day with plenty of tables to go around.

The bottom line when it comes to avoiding double agent situations is trust. Companies that distrust their customers and employees end up creating rigid policies that cause employees to get stuck between a rock and a hard place. On the other hand, companies that emphasize trust, generosity, and goodwill almost always create more positive and profitable relationships between their employees and customers.

Weighing Risk vs. Reward

When customer service employees feel caught between their employer and their customer, their actions may be decided by their perception of risk vs. reward. On one hand, they can follow the employer's policies and avoid getting into trouble with their boss, but this course of action may risk angering the customer. On the other hand, they can side with the customer and be rewarded with the customer's gratitude, but then they risk getting into trouble for violating the company's policy.

Employees experiencing conflict in double agent situations tend to be influenced by two factors:

1. Whether their actions are monitored
2. What the consequences are for pleasing or displeasing each principal

Employees are more likely to side with their employer over the customer if their actions are being monitored and they are at risk for being reprimanded. Call center employees tend to be sticklers to company policy since many of their calls are recorded and reviewed. Employees who work in close proximity to their supervisor know their supervisor may be watching them at any given time. Any transaction that results in an electronic record also increases the chances that a double agent employee will side with the company.

Returning the shredder at the office supply store required a transaction that would be captured in the store's computer. Toeing the line and refusing a shredder return makes sense from the employee's perspective because a refund for a shredder is likely to be noticed. The store's computer may have even required a manager override to approve the transaction, so the employee couldn't do it without the manager's knowledge.

Employees' risk vs. reward calculation may change when they are not easily monitored. Employees who work autonomously or whose work is not digitally monitored are less likely to be observed by their supervisor.

Double agent employees may be more likely to side with their customers if they think they won't get caught.

My wife and I often bring our own bottle of wine when dining at a restaurant. This is fairly common practice in California, where many people are wine enthusiasts and liquor laws allow it. Restaurants typically charge a $15 to $25 corkage fee to open and serve the wine, which is usually much less than the markup on wine purchased from the restaurant. The corkage fee ensures restaurant owners will still make a nice profit, even though customers aren't buying the wine from them. Over the years, though, I've observed that servers waive the corkage fee nearly 20 percent of the time. We don't ask them to waive the fee; it just doesn't appear on the bill. This happens even more when we're regular guests at the restaurant and have gotten to know the servers, or when we are dining with a larger group and bring in more than one bottle.

Waiving the fee saves us money, but it costs the restaurant revenue. So why do they do it?

The decision to waive the corkage fee may come down to the incentives and disincentives that guide a double agent's behavior. Unlike a shredder return at the office supply store, where all transactions are recorded in the store's computerized cash registers, the restaurant's corkage fee is harder to monitor. Since we're bringing in our own bottle, no wine comes out of the restaurant's stock. Also, drinking wine with the meal that we've ordered doesn't necessarily signal that a corkage fee is in order.

This leads to the second factor that influences an employee's risk vs. reward calculation—the consequences involved. Restaurant corkage fees can generate complaints from customers who aren't used to the practice or who believe the fee is too high. On the other hand, waiving the corkage fee is an easy way for our server to give us a little something extra with our meal. It's a good chance we'll be happier with the service and increase the server's tip correspondingly.

Employees will sometimes engage in unethical or even illegal behavior when their actions are unmonitored and the rewards are great enough. A nightclub bouncer could put the club's liquor license at risk if he lets in an underage drinker, but a small bribe might get him to look the other way if a manager isn't watching. These bribes might add up to become a significant source of income and could outweigh any fear of getting caught and losing his job.

Companies can do several things to help their employees make better decisions in situations where their customers' demands seem at odds with the organization's best interests. As discussed previously in this chapter, the first step is to institute more customer-friendly policies. Employees have less incentive to act on their own when their company's interests are aligned with the customers'.

Let's look back at restaurant corkage fees. Many restaurants have eliminated this problem by opening a small wine shop or partnering with a local wine merchant to offer a wide selection of wine at reasonable retail prices. One of my favorite restaurants in San Diego, Cucina Urbana, charges a modest $7 fee to open a bottle of wine purchased at its store. This policy encourages more customers to buy wine from the restaurant rather than bring their own. Since customers generally like this policy, servers feel less pressure to waive the small fee to prevent complaints.

Nevertheless, careful monitoring is important to give employees less incentive to act on their own. When I worked for a parking management company, we often increased revenue by 30 percent or more when we took over a parking garage from a competitor. Our secret was a rigorous auditing process that discouraged employee theft and ensured customers were charged the appropriate parking fee. People don't like to pay for parking, so complaints were a natural part of the business, but employees knew they would be caught if they gave in to the demands of an unreasonable customer and lowered or dropped the fee.

Training is another way to prevent employees from becoming double agents. There are certain situations, like charging a parking fee, where it may be impossible to align the company's and the customer's interests.

Employees who have the skills to effectively handle tricky situations are less likely to give in to a customer's unreasonable demands.

One of the best techniques employees can learn is to provide options instead of saying "No." The word *no* can trigger a customer's anger because it makes her feel powerless. Providing options is usually more acceptable since it invites the customer's cooperation. For example, at the parking company, I trained attendants to give customers the option of paying the full fee or going back into the building to get their parking validated when applicable. Customers were much less likely to get upset when it was their choice, and most of them chose to pay the full fee rather than spend extra time obtaining a validation just to save a few dollars.

Getting Employees to Do the Dirty Work

The television show *Undercover Boss* exposes an interesting bit of workplace psychology: It's easier for bosses to ask an employee to do something unpopular than it is for them do it themselves.

In each episode of the show, an executive dons a disguise to avoid being recognized and goes "undercover" to shadow employees working frontline positions in his or her own company. The boss's goals for participating in the show usually include seeing if executive decisions are truly being carried out on the frontlines. During the show, the bosses almost always make surprising discoveries about the quality and consequences of those decisions.

One episode featured Michael Rubin, CEO of GSI Commerce. GSI Commerce provides marketing, customer service, and order fulfillment services to help companies like Major League Baseball sell merchandise. Rubin found himself squarely in the middle of the double agent problem during a segment where he took customer calls in the escalations department of one of the company's call centers.

An upset customer called because she discovered she was being charged $149 for a $99 item. The customer wanted to pay the correct price of $99 but was told the company policy was to charge her $149 and then issue a $50 credit to fix the error after the item had shipped. Her call had been transferred to the escalations department, and now Rubin had to handle the irate caller.

The undercover CEO struggled. Simple logic dictated that the customer should pay the correct price, but his own company policy didn't allow him to make this adjustment. The customer's anger, coupled with his inability to do anything about it, left him at a loss for words. Danielle, the call center employee he was shadowing, had to step in and take over the call.

Danielle was now facing the double agent dilemma. Unaware that she was sitting next to the company CEO, she resorted to treating the customer rudely.[5] At one point she informed Rubin that the way to handle the customer was to sound confident and "put her in her place."

Unfortunately for Danielle, Rubin was able to step back into the role of CEO when she took over the call from him. His focus shifted from the obvious discomfort of the double agent dilemma to annoyance at how rudely Danielle was treating the customer. Danielle's performance, not the restrictive policy, became the focus of his attention.

Each *Undercover Boss* episode ends with a segment where the employees the boss has shadowed are called to the corporate office. Here they discover whom they were actually working with. During this segment, Rubin reprimanded Danielle for her performance and told her that he was going to have her retrained. He made no mention of addressing the policy that caused the problem in the first place.

John Hamman, George Loewenstein, and Roberto Weber are social scientists at Carnegie Mellon University who discovered a possible explanation for Rubin's behavior. They conducted an experiment where participants were given $10 and instructed to share as much of it as they'd like with another participant. Next, they were asked to repeat the experiment, but this time they used an intermediary (i.e., an employee) to share the money on their behalf. On average, participants shared $1 less when using an intermediary than when they shared the money directly.[6]

The implication of the experiment—and of the *Undercover Boss* segment—is that unfavorable or unethical policies are easier for managers to implement if they don't have to carry them out themselves. Insulated from angry customers and frustrated frontline employees, executives turn to data such as financial statements, cost/benefit analysis, and other tools to make decisions that impact customer service. Executives who are really out of touch may dismiss any negative feedback as the viewpoint of a small minority rather than something to be legitimately concerned about.

Bank of America grabbed headlines in September 2011 when the bank announced it would begin charging customers a $5 monthly fee for making purchases with their debit card.[7] Consumer outcry was loud and swift, but CEO Brian Moynihan initially defended the decision as being in the best interests of the company and its shareholders. In an interview with CNBC's Larry Kudlow, Moynihan explained that the fees were an effort by the bank to be transparent and up front with its customers while maximizing profitability. Moynihan was insistent that the decision to implement the fee was made only after gathering extensive feedback from customers, and he was convinced that customers would accept the fee in the long run.[8]

However, Bank of America faced a wave of criticism from its customers in the month that followed. One customer collected 153,000 signatures on a petition denouncing the fee.[9] The Credit Union National Association released a study that suggested as many as 650,000 customers had transferred their accounts to a credit union in response to fees at Bank of America and other institutions.[10] Protesters even organized a nationwide Bank Transfer Day to encourage people to move their accounts in response to new bank fees.

Moynihan was undoubtedly aware of the bad press, and he repeatedly had to answer questions about the $5 fee as he made the rounds on the talk show circuit. What he didn't have to do was spend his day working face-to-face with the bank's angry customers. That was left to the tellers, the call center representatives, and other employees who were on the frontlines of customer service.

Ultimately, Bank of America relented to the growing pressure and dropped its plans to implement the $5 monthly debit card fee. In an interview published in the *Boston Globe,* Moynihan admitted the fee was a mistake: "We didn't do our best work there. We did a lot of testing, but the customer spoke and we pulled it back."[11]

My own bank, a Bank of America competitor, also raised fees in 2011 that drove customers to other banks. Customer after customer came in to close their accounts or complain about the new fees, and this constant criticism began to wear on the bank's frontline employees. Several employees told me that they felt frustrated and powerless because the bank had sent letters to customers to explain the fees, but they were the ones who had to field the complaints, try to justify the decision, and make what was often a futile attempt to retain the customer's business.

The solution to avoid being insulated from customers is quite simple. Executives must spend time on the frontlines to see what is really going on in their operations. They should listen directly to customers and frontline employees so that their decision making is influenced by real feedback and not just aggregate numbers on a spreadsheet or a slick presentation from the marketing department. They should observe their operations to see if employees are truly delivering the kind of service they expect their customers to receive. And they should take time to carefully explain strategic decisions and policy changes, so employees have an opportunity to understand and embrace their leader's vision.

This leadership approach is sometimes referred to as "management by walking around" and has been practiced by many legendary customer service leaders. Walt Disney, Bill Marriott, and In-N-Out founder Harry Snyder were all famous for their willingness to view their business from the ground level to understand what was really happening. William Rosenberg, the founder of the Dunkin' Donuts franchise, tirelessly visited his franchisees to ensure their food quality and customer service met his exacting standards. He was even known to dump out a batch of coffee if it wasn't fresh enough when he visited a Dunkin' Donuts store.[12]

Solution Summary: Avoiding the Creation of Double Agents

The double agent problem comes from a conflict between the company and the customer, with the employee stuck in the middle. The ultimate solution for any company trying to provide outstanding customer service is to identify these harmful pressures and neutralize them as much as possible. It should be easy and natural for an employee to *want* to do the right thing for both the customer and the company.

Here is a short summary of specific ways to help employees avoid becoming double agents:

- Avoid policies that are certain to anger customers and require your employees to face their displeasure.

- Whenever possible, allow employees to use their discretion when carrying out corporate policies; give them the flexibility to meet the needs of the company and the customer.

- Look beyond a single transaction to consider the lifetime value of a customer when setting restrictive policies or implementing new fees.

- Trust that the vast majority of your employees and customers are not trying to take advantage of you.

- Make sure employees are adequately monitored so that you can guide their performance.

- Identify and eliminate incentives that may cause employees to act against the company's best interests.

- Spend considerable time interacting with employees and customers, to avoid becoming insulated from reality when making policy decisions.

Notes

1. Susan R. Ellis, Siegfried P. Gudergan, and Lester W. Johnson, "The Satisfaction Mirror as a Principal-Agent Problem," paper presented at the ANZMAC (Australian and New Zealand Marketing Academy) Conference, December 1, 2000.

2. The Retail Owners Institute (www.retailowner.com), 2010 figures. I also reviewed financial statements from Office Depot, Staples, and Office Max and verified this approximation of gross margin as reasonably accurate for the purposes of this discussion.

3. Michael Arndt, "L.L.Bean Follows Its Shoppers to the Web," *Bloomberg Businessweek,* March 1, 2010.

4. "Guaranteed to Last" return policy, www.llbean.com.

5. Danielle was interviewed by Roy A. Barnes for a Yahoo! blog. In the interview, Danielle said the actual call lasted about ten minutes, but portions of the call were not aired on the show. The blog post is available at http://voices.yahoo.com/undercover-boss-gsi-commerce-episode-5702070.html.

6. John R. Hamman, George Loewenstein, and Roberto A. Weber, "Self-Interest Through Delegation: An Additional Rationale for the Principal-Agent Relationship," *American Economic Review* 100, no. 4 (September 2010), pp. 1826–1846, http://sds.hss.cmu.edu/media/pdfs/loewenstein/Self-InterestThruDelegation.pdf.

7. Blake Ellis, "Bank of America to Charge $5 Monthly Debit Card Fee," *CNNMoney.com,* September 29, 2011.

8. Jennifer Liberto, "BofA Chief: We Have a 'Right to Make a Profit,'" *CNNMoney.com,* October 5, 2011.

9. Devin Dwyer, "Bank of America Customer Delivers 153,000 Signatures in Petition Over Fee," ABC News Blogs, October 6, 2011.

10. Credit Union National Association, "Rising Fees at Banks Spark Consumer Action During October in Run-up to 'Bank Transfer Day,'" news release, November 3, 2011.

11. Todd Wallack and Shirley Leung, "Moynihan: 'Our Job Is to Be Fair to Consumers,'" *Boston Globe,* December 21, 2011.

12. William Rosenberg with Jessica Brilliant Keener, *Time to Make the Donuts* (New York: Lebhar-Friedman Books, 2001).

CHAPTER 5

Mutually Assured Dissatisfaction

Getting Beyond Broken Systems
That Cause Employee Disengagement

I t's never a good sign when a customer service representative uses the word *they* to refer to her own company. It indicates the employee is disassociating herself from her employer, and it often means you're about to receive poor service.

When I had to ship my malfunctioning laptop back to the manufacturer, so it could be repaired under warranty, it was frustrating enough to lose the use of a new computer. My laptop was expected to be returned within three days, but then I received an e-mail from the company telling me a part needed to make the repair was on backorder. Even worse, the repairs department didn't know when the backordered part would arrive.

I called the customer service line and a representative named Sherry answered the phone. She was polite, friendly, and empathetic. Unfortunately, she wasn't able to give me an update on the status of my computer. She told me that my only option was to wait six days and call again.

"*They* won't let me escalate it until it's been six business days. I tried to escalate it sooner, once before, and *they* told me it was too early."

Sherry didn't offer any alternatives, so I suggested a couple of my own. I asked if they could take the needed part from another computer or perhaps just send me a new computer, since they couldn't tell me when they'd be able to repair mine. The answer to both of my suggestions was, "No." According to Sherry, she had tried those routes already; her response was, "They told me they aren't able to do it."

I was disappointed and frustrated, but I suspect Sherry was, too. After all, she didn't manufacture my laptop improperly, she didn't cause the parts shortage, she wasn't responsible for the lack of information on the backordered part, and she clearly didn't write the policy that makes customers wait six business days before escalating the inquiry to someone with greater authority and resources.

Many people get into customer service because they like to help others, but Sherry wasn't being given the opportunity to provide that help. Instead, she was tasked with sharing bad news without being able to offer any solutions. I could tell from the tone in her voice that she'd probably taken a lot of calls such as mine.

This chapter explores the critical link between a company's service delivery systems and its employees' motivation. We'll learn how employees can be put in an impossible position when those systems are broken. Eventually, employees may stop trying, and they may even begin to work against your company's best interests. When customer service leaders don't discover or rectify problems that are hindering employee performance, those problems can continue unchecked.

Broken Systems Lead to Disengaged Employees

John Goodman of TARP Worldwide estimates that as much as 60 percent of customer dissatisfaction is a result of poor products, services, or processes.[1] Unfortunately for customer service employees, they're usually the ones who bear the brunt of the customer's anger. Rationally, this is part of their job. Emotionally, it's difficult to repeatedly take the blame for something that's completely out of your control.

Examples abound. Customers who call a 1-800 number and spend ten minutes navigating through endless menu options are probably going to be frustrated by the time they reach a live person. The cable company may do a poor job of managing work schedules, but it's the repair technician who has to face the fuming customer when he arrives an hour later than expected. A customer waiting in unbelievably long lines at the Department of Motor Vehicles is likely to be somewhat agitated by the time she reaches the employee behind the counter.

Customer service representatives are often part of a much larger system that serves a company's customers. This system is made up of people from various departments, policies and procedures, and the leaders who design and manage them all. When these systems are broken, frontline employees may lack the resources or authority to resolve the issues that lead to poor service. In many cases, these employees are just as frustrated as their customers because they must repeatedly listen to complaints while being powerless to help.

Sherry, the customer service rep at the computer manufacturer, was caught in a broken system when she explained to me her company's far-flung operations. The backordered part needed to fix my computer was being shipped from a supplier in Asia. The facility that would complete the repair once the part finally arrived was located in Memphis. Sherry worked at the company's call center in Atlanta. As much as she wanted to help me, any action she suggested would have to be reviewed, approved, and executed by someone else in a different department and in a different city. Repairing and returning my computer was physically out of her control.

Situations like these are made worse when customers make no distinction between the employee and the company. A customer who says, "You screwed up my order" or "You can't do anything right" may be referring to the company, but the language and tone feel like a personal attack to the employee. Employees soon find themselves in a no-win situation where they can't fix the problem and yet they feel like they are receiving all the blame.

I saw this problem firsthand when I worked as a training supervisor for the call center of a clothing catalog company. One of the company's broken systems was handling returned merchandise. The returns department was so chronically behind that packages sent back by customers would sit for up to four weeks in a truck trailer behind the warehouse before employees even opened the packages and recorded the returns in the customer database.

This created an information void that caused big problems for customer service reps. Reps had to rely on the database when customers called to inquire about the status of their return, but the reps couldn't give an answer if the returned merchandise hadn't been recorded in the database yet. Customers were understandably upset when told the company had no idea whether a return they'd mailed three weeks ago had arrived.

The company also had some unfriendly return policies that made customers even angrier. Customers returning an item they didn't want couldn't receive a refund until the return had been recorded. Customers who wanted to exchange an item would have to be charged for the new item if they didn't want to wait the three to four weeks for their exchange to be processed. These inflexible policies made it even more difficult for customer service reps to provide a solution.

My department was asked to train the call center representatives to handle these situations as best they could, but implementing a few communication techniques was no substitute for fixing the real problem. I don't know of any secret phrase that can make a customer feel better when your business is unable to find a package mailed three weeks earlier, and then it is unwilling to help the customer until after it has finally processed the return. Needless to say, our training was of little help.

Our customer service reps were incredibly frustrated by their inability to provide any real assistance to these customers. Eventually, either they learned to stop caring or they left the job. The employees who remained became less and less empathetic to their customers as they grew tired of repeatedly handling the same complaints. Many of the employees who didn't quit were eventually fired for poor performance.

The vice president of customer service finally tried to address the problem by instituting a process improvement initiative called "One Call Resolution." The goal: Resolve customer complaints on the very first call, so customers wouldn't call us over and over about the same problem. But the entire initiative consisted of a banner hung in a conference room and a short meeting to explain the concept to our call center supervisors. Nothing was done to address the huge backlog of unprocessed returns and the inflexible policies, which remained unchanged.

In his landmark book *Good to Great,* bestselling author and researcher Jim Collins examined why some companies make the leap to greatness while others don't. One of his findings was that great companies have leaders who are continually on the lookout for systemic problems.[2] Conversely, companies that wallow in mediocrity or eventually fail often do so because of their inability or unwillingness to identify and confront these challenges.

Organizations that consistently identify and fix service delivery problems go way beyond hanging a banner or holding a pep rally. They monitor service levels, conduct a root-cause analysis to find the source of problems, and rapidly implement real solutions. Employees at all levels, from the frontlines to top executives, are focused on continually improving customer service.

Oregon's Portland International Airport is an example of an organization that consistently roots out systematic issues that can impact customer service. The results have paid off. In 2010, *Condé Nast Traveler* rated it the best airport in the United States for the fourth time in five years.[3]

Donna Prigmore is the customer relations manager at Portland International Airport. She and other airport leaders ask a lot of questions and regularly engage in dialogue with employees and passengers in an effort to capture customer feedback and identify any potential problems. Donna speaks with employees who work for the airlines, restaurants, stores, and service providers operating at the airport. She talks to passengers directly and solicits their feedback via a customer service survey. She even checks in with the volunteers who work at the airport's information booth to learn what questions are asked most often and what problems travelers encounter most frequently.

When a problem is identified, Donna and her team are able to bring the airport's various departments, vendors, and contractors together to find a solution. For example, when some of the employees who help passengers find a taxi or hotel shuttle overheard several people complaining about all the restrooms in the baggage claim area being closed, they forwarded this feedback to Donna, who shared the information with the janitorial department supervisor. This supervisor adjusted the cleaning schedule accordingly, to prevent all the restrooms in one area from being closed at the same time. It was a small issue, but one that could have been difficult to resolve unless someone like Donna was able to connect all of the pieces.

Learned Helplessness Arises from Broken Systems

The longer systemic service failures are allowed to continue, the more likely employees are to become frustrated and dissatisfied with their jobs. Employees in this situation may soon find themselves thinking, "They don't pay me enough to deal with this every day."

Broken systems can eventually lead employees to experience a condition that psychologists call learned helplessness. It occurs when people believe they are powerless to stop something negative from happening—and so they begin to act as if it were a foregone conclusion.[4] Employees suffering from learned helplessness stop trying to resolve problems or provide outstanding service because they believe there's nothing they can do to make the customer happy.

Sherry, the computer manufacturer's customer service rep, was experiencing learned helplessness. She explained all the reasons why she was unable to help me get my computer repaired and returned any quicker. Her attitude was that there was nothing that could be done but wait. Any suggestion I made was quickly countered with, "I've tried that before and it won't work."

Employees experiencing learned helplessness also tend to become focused on placing blame for their dissatisfaction rather than trying to resolve it. They blame management for not fixing the broken system or process. They blame other departments for not doing their jobs correctly. Some may even blame their customers for not being more understanding.

I once stepped into an airport newsstand to buy a magazine. While I was searching for one that looked interesting, I overheard the newsstand's two employees trying to outdo each other with stories of poor customer behavior. Their stories all started with some version of "What I hate about customers is . . ." It became obvious that I would likely become more fodder for them, so I left the store without making a purchase.

You'd expect employees to leave their jobs if they disliked them so much, but people experiencing learned helplessness may not realize this is an option. I returned to the same airport newsstand three months later and encountered the same two employees having the same conversation about customers they hate. This time, I was determined to have something to read for my flight, so I quickly selected a magazine and took it to the register. The two employees looked at me disdainfully while one of them rang up my purchase. I waited patiently for her to tell me the total, but she instead pointed at the display on her register without saying a word. I paid the amount indicated and as I left the store I overheard the employees complaining about customers who are too dumb to see the amount displayed on the register.

When employees believe that customer dissatisfaction is a foregone conclusion, it becomes a self-reinforcing concept. Because these employees have stopped trying to fix problems they don't think can be solved, customers continue to get irritated with both the problem and the employee. The customer's unhappiness further reinforces the employee's belief that dissatisfaction is inevitable.

The best way to help employees avoid experiencing learned helplessness is to make them feel like a valuable part of your organization's efforts to continually improve customer service. Ask for their feedback. Involve them in process improvement initiatives. Give them the skills and authority to take greater control of the service they provide.

Employees will help you identify the source of service failures when they know their input is expected and their suggestions are listened to. People working at the Portland International Airport are continually on the lookout for opportunities to improve customer service because that's part of the culture. They know their observations count and, most important, their suggestions will be taken seriously.

Involving employees in process improvement initiatives is another important step. I once worked with a client's payroll department to help the staff members overcome learned helplessness by involving them in improving their processes. The department had been under scrutiny for extensive errors and frequently missing or delayed paychecks. Department employees had become so busy trying to keep up with their workload that they were convinced the only solution was to add additional employees. However, there was no room in the budget to bring on more staff, so the team began to accept the errors and delays as inevitable.

Our first step together was coming to an agreement on the role of the department. Payroll viewed its function as a data-processing center, where time cards went in and paychecks came out. This task-oriented approach made it difficult for the payroll staff to distinguish between essential and nonessential tasks or to appreciate how frustrating it was for employees not to receive paychecks or be paid less than they were owed. The payroll team needed to view employees as internal customers, so we redefined the team's role to focus on ensuring all employees were paid accurately and on time.

The second step was to create a map of the current payroll process. They instinctively knew that some of their work was inefficient, but this map helped them visualize some glaring problems. They were able to identify many duplicate steps that could be eliminated. Reflecting on their vision of paying all employees accurately and on time also helped the team reprioritize work so that nonessential tasks were put aside during busy times. Finally, the team implemented several safeguards against errors so that fewer employees would receive incorrect paychecks and the payroll team would spend less time fixing mistakes.

The final step was to implement the new procedures and measure progress. The entire team was eager to try out the new process that it had created and felt much better about its ability to achieve great results. The team's efforts and positive attitude resulted in a 25 percent reduction in payroll processing time, a sharp reduction in errors, and a savings of thousands of dollars. The department gradually began earning back the trust of internal customers. Best of all, the payroll team now realized it could control its own success and wasn't dependent on adding additional employees to be successful.

Employees may not always be able to fix a broken system, but they still may have the ability to influence a better outcome for their customers. A call center representative may not be able to get returns processed any faster, but he may be allowed to send out a replacement order before the returned merchandise is received. An employee at an airport newsstand may not be able to control the long security lines that aggravate travelers, but she can try to brighten another person's day with an infectious smile and fast, friendly service.

The Dangers of Employee Disengagement

Employee engagement is defined as the extent to which employees purposefully contribute to their organization's success. According to the BlessingWhite 2011 Employee Engagement Report, fully 18 percent of U.S.

employees are *dis*engaged—meaning they're dissatisfied with both their jobs and the companies they work for. The report says these employees "are the most disconnected from organizational priorities, often feel underutilized, and are clearly not getting what they need from work."[5]

There are many reasons an employee may become disengaged. The employee may have been hired to do a job she doesn't enjoy. The employee may have a poor relationship with his boss. One of the biggest contributors to employee disengagement is a failure to detect and fix processes that produce customer dissatisfaction.

Chronic customer service failure can trip several levers that contribute to employee disengagement. Employees may feel as though their contributions don't count since they don't have the ability to improve the broken process. They may feel their voice isn't heard if their manager doesn't listen to or act on feedback about chronically broken systems. They can easily be discouraged after repeatedly being on the receiving end of customer complaints they come to believe they aren't able to resolve.

You can imagine how unlikely it is to get even passable customer service from someone who's disengaged from his work and employer. This kind of employee simply doesn't care about serving customers and gives the minimal amount of effort just to get by. Some of these employees intentionally deliver poor service as a means of lashing out at their employer and customers.

JetBlue flight attendant Steven Slater suddenly became famous in August 2010 for committing what is easily described as an ultimate act of employee disengagement. The incident occurred aboard a JetBlue plane on the tarmac of New York's John F. Kennedy International Airport. After an apparent argument with a passenger, Slater reportedly got on the plane's public address system and let loose a string of expletives. He then grabbed a beer from the plane's galley, opened an exit door, and slid down an emergency slide.[6]

Ironically, Slater received an outpouring of support from other customer service employees who viewed themselves as equally fed up with their customers' boorish behavior. They hailed Slater as a hero for doing what many had always imagined themselves doing. Meanwhile, JetBlue was faced with an embarrassing public relations incident, an employee facing criminal charges, and a costly repair job to fix the emergency slide on the airplane.

This may be an extreme example, but there are many other instances where disengaged employees deliberately provide poor service. A retail associate may avoid customers who are obviously in search of help. A restaurant server may keep customers waiting while she carries on a conversation with a coworker. A city worker may intentionally delay processing paperwork needed for a building permit.

Employee disengagement can also make it more costly for companies to deliver customer service. Gallup, another organization that measures employee engagement, estimates that disengaged employees in the United States alone cost companies $300 billion annually in lost productivity.[7] When I worked as a training supervisor for the catalog company with the returns problems, chronic absenteeism and high turnover rates were two costs related to employee disengagement that directly affected the bottom line.

On any given day, nearly 20 percent of the company's call center employees would call in sick. The company had to hire extra employees and pay expensive overtime to cover shifts for the absentees. Supervisors spent a lot of their time disciplining employees for absenteeism, which in turn created additional resentment.

The cost of excessive turnover was also substantial. The company's annual turnover rate among call center employees was well over 100 percent. Most employees quit or were fired before they had been there even one full year, and many didn't even make it ninety days. This created a continual need to hire and train new employees, which significantly elevated recruiting and training costs. Furthermore, the high turnover rate gave the company a reputation in the community as an undesirable place to work, so it soon became much harder to find talented—and engaged—employees.

At the opposite end of the spectrum are engaged employees, and according to BlessingWhite's 2011 Employee Engagement Report, 33 percent of U.S. workers fall in this category. Engaged customer service employees understand and agree with their company's goals, strategies, and attitudes toward customer service. These employees consistently try to align their performance with the needs of their employer.[8]

This research suggests employers need two essential elements to engage their customer service employees. First, customer service leaders must share their customer service goals with employees and provide feedback on progress toward those goals. Second, employees must be enlisted as partners in achieving these goals rather than being treated as pawns who move at management's whim.

Enterprise Rent-A-Car is an organization that has leveraged employee engagement to earn a reputation for outstanding customer service. At the heart of its engagement efforts is the Enterprise Service Quality Index (ESQi), which is a system used to evaluate customer satisfaction. Enterprise customers are regularly surveyed on their rental experience, and the results are captured and reported at the local branch level.[9]

The ESQi results are regularly reported throughout the company. Employees are trained on the factors that drive customer satisfaction. They are encouraged to use their discretion to fix problems on the spot in an effort to avoid poor survey scores. A relentless desire to improve service has even spurred innovative ideas from frontline employees, such as Enterprise's most famous service offering to pick you up at your home or office.[10]

Leaders Blind to Reality

By now, you may be wondering why more companies don't fix the broken systems that hurt customer service and crush employee engagement.

This is precisely the area where leaders in many organizations fall short. Some leaders rely too much on reports and data, rather than listening to employees and customers. Others just assume that employees will perform better if they're given more incentives or face stiffer sanctions. Like employees, some leaders simply don't care.

Dave, an account manager for a company that sold uniforms, was a good example of what can happen to customer service employees when their managers are blind to the root causes of poor service. His job was to take orders, provide customer service, and find ways to increase sales with each of his customers.

Business hadn't been very good for Dave and his coworkers. Sales were down, customer complaints were up, and many customers were taking their business to competitors. Like many of his coworkers, Dave began to exhibit signs of learned helplessness and disengagement. He spent a good part of his day commiserating with coworkers about slumping sales, taking extra-long breaks, and finding ways to avoid work altogether.

Dave's manager knew he needed to turn things around. When he looked at the department's sales reports to find the answer, it seemed to jump out almost immediately. The company's phone call tracking software revealed that Dave and most of his coworkers were making far fewer phone calls than they had been just three months earlier, when the sales figures were much better. The manager knew that taking care of customers required frequent contact, so the solution seemed obvious. The account managers needed to make more calls!

The next Monday, the manager announced a special incentive program. Any account manager who made 125 phone calls by the end of the week would earn a $100 cash bonus.

The plan worked wonderfully. All the account managers made at least 125 calls and earned the $100 bonus. Dave, whose calls had gone down significantly in recent months, reached 125 calls by Thursday! The manager patted himself on the back as employee after employee complimented him on a great incentive program.

The only problem was that sales didn't go up during that week. In fact, sales actually went *down* from the week before. Dave's manager was convinced the incentive program was a great plan, so he couldn't understand what had happened.

Dave knew why (and after reading the passage in Chapter 3 about the problem with financial incentives, you may have guessed why, too). Dave earned the $100 bonus, but not by calling customers. Instead, he called friends, family members, and even dialed his own number a few times to make sure the call tracking software recorded 125 phone calls.

Dave didn't call many customers because he knew there was nothing to talk about. His customers had been upset for the past year about long lead times and quality issues. The last straw had come three months ago, when the company significantly raised its prices. Now Dave's products were more expensive, took longer to ship, and had more errors per order than those sold by his competitors.

Dave began exhibiting signs of disengagement and learned helplessness as more and more customers defected and sales declined. He made fewer phone calls because he was tired of fielding complaints about high prices and poor quality. Dave had gone to his manager for help, but the manager didn't seem to listen. In a typical disengagement pattern, Dave began spending most of his day complaining to coworkers while waiting for things to somehow get better.

The manager never questioned why a successful and experienced account manager like Dave suddenly stopped making calls. It never occurred to the manager that the increase in prices had taken away Dave's last remaining competitive advantage. Now the company's customers were leaving in droves to buy better-quality products that were delivered faster for less money.

Managers who remain blind to the big picture aren't likely to solve the systemic problems that drive customers away. Too often, leaders fail to dig deeper when they encounter the symptoms of poor service. They try simple fixes—such as offering incentives, trying to script employees' behaviors, or even threatening employees with disciplinary action or termination—which only create more problems. What these leaders don't do often enough is carefully examine the real root cause of the problem before creating a solution.

Successful customer service leaders approach problems by first asking questions. They resist the urge to assign blame, jump to conclusions, or dismiss the problem altogether and instead try to understand what's really going on. It doesn't have to be a lengthy process; they are just careful to face reality before designing and implementing solutions.

One of my favorite exercises to use in this situation is to imagine an iceberg. Only the tip of an iceberg is visible above the surface of the water, but what lies unseen is often bigger and more dangerous. Uncovering icebergs usually involves asking just a few questions when confronted with a service problem:

- Is it possible this same problem has happened before?
- How likely is it that this problem will happen again?
- Can similar problems exist in other places?
- Who else might be affected by this problem?
- What can I learn from this problem that can be applied to other issues?

I remember conducting an iceberg investigation when I was customer service manager for a catalog company that was plagued by backorders on a popular product. My customer service reps were being besieged with calls from angry customers, and it was definitely taking a toll on their morale. It was tempting to write off the backorders as a simple matter of demand far exceeding supply, but this did little to help my employees provide better service.

The questions in the iceberg framework took me to many places within the company, from merchandising, to information technology, to our warehouse and order fulfillment operations. Working closely with managers from these departments we discovered a host of problems. These problems had far wider implications than a single product, but they also illuminated opportunities for improvement.

The whole process generated a list of solutions that may never have been discovered without looking for icebergs. We implemented a system where we proactively communicated updates to our customers on backordered products, using phone calls, e-mails, and postcards, which greatly reduced customer inquiries. Our information technology team discovered and repaired a computer glitch that miscalculated inventory levels and often made it appear that an item was in stock when it really wasn't. The order fulfillment team improved its inventory tracking procedures and discovered large quantities of backordered products that had been previously lost in the warehouse.

Customer satisfaction is clearly linked to a company's ability to deal with operational problems head-on. In *Good to Great*, Jim Collins aptly describes this as a willingness to "confront the brutal facts."[11] The process may be painful, but the long-term payoff is customer service delivery systems that work.

Solution Summary: Avoiding Mutually Assured Dissatisfaction

The best customer service organizations make it incredibly easy, instead of impossibly hard, for their employees to provide outstanding service. Here is a summary of the solutions presented in this chapter:

- Take action to identify and address operational issues that contribute to customer service failures and frustrate employees.
- Include employees in your organization's efforts to continually improve customer service.
- Engage employees by sharing customer service goals, then enlisting employees' help toward achieving them.

- Avoid becoming blind to reality by avidly searching for icebergs—the small signs that could be indicators of big problems.

- Approach operational problems by asking questions and gaining a true understanding of what's going on before jumping to conclusions about the solution.

Notes

1. John Goodman, "Basic Facts on Customer Complaint Behavior and the Impact of Service on the Bottom Line," *Competitive Advantage* 9, no 1 (June 1999), pp. 1–5.

2. Jim Collins, *Good to Great: Why Some Companies Make the Leap and Others Don't* (New York: HarperBusiness, 2001).

3. "The 13th Annual Business Travel Awards," *Condé Nast Traveler,* October 2010.

4. Guy Winch, *The Squeaky Wheel: Complaining the Right Way to Get Results, Improve Your Relationships, and Enhance Self-Esteem* (New York: Walker Publishing, 2011).

5. "Employee Engagement Report 2011, *Beyond the Numbers: A Practical Approach for Individuals, Managers, and Executives*" BlessingWhite white paper, January 2011; available at www.blessingwhite.com/EEE__report.asp.

6. Sean Gardiner, "Flight Attendant Pops Emergency Chute, Escapes Plane at JFK," *Wall Street Journal,* August 9, 2010.

7. John H. Fleming, Curt Coffman, and James K. Harter, "Manage Your Human Sigma," *Harvard Business Review* (July–August 2005), pp. 107–114.

8. "Employee Engagement Report 2011," BlessingWhite white paper.

9. An overview of ESQi can be found on the Enterprise Rent-A-Car website; see http://aboutus.enterprise.com/customer_service.html.

10. Fred Reichheld, *The Ultimate Question 2.0* (Boston: Harvard Business School Publishing, 2011).

11. Jim Collins, *Good to Great.*

(F)

CHAPTER 6

Conformity Is Contagious

Creating a Company Culture That Encourages
Outstanding Customer Service

I go to In-N-Out Burger a lot. The law of averages suggests I should have had a bad experience at least once by now. Some visits have been better than others, but I've never had a bad experience. Not one.

I'm not alone in my admiration of In-N-Out. It's consistently ranked among the top fast-food chains in customer satisfaction.[1] The chain has locations in only a handful of states, but people all over the country and even outside the United States have become fans, with some devoted followers even planning a business trip or vacation itinerary around a visit to an In-N-Out establishment.

What's the secret to In-N-Out's success? It may be easier to understand if you compare the chain to a similar restaurant that struggles with customer service: McDonald's.[2]

The two have a lot in common. While McDonald's has a more diverse menu, both chains are fundamentally fast-food burger joints. Both were founded in Southern California in 1948. Many fast-food service concepts in use today originated at either In-N-Out or McDonald's. The two companies even use the same three words as a foundation of their operating principles: quality, service, and cleanliness.[3]

So why is the customer service experience at these two restaurants so different? In a word: *culture.* Culture defines everything these organizations do when it comes to customer service.

In-N-Out founder Harry Snyder made sure the principles of "quality, cleanliness, and service" were more than just platitudes. He instilled them in everything the company did—and these principles are still present in everything In-N-Out does today. The food is fresh, not frozen. The stores are clean, even during busy times. Employees are friendly and well-trained. In-N-Out has maintained remarkable consistency by steadfastly refusing to franchise its stores and resisting the urge to expand too quickly.

Culture also shapes many other business practices, such as hiring. In-N-Out's management believes a high-caliber employee is necessary to provide the service and quality that customers expect. In-N-Out offers better wages and working conditions than its competitors, which contributes to one of the lowest employee turnover rates in the fast-food industry.[4]

When Ray Kroc purchased the McDonald's concept from the McDonald brothers, he focused on rapidly expanding the business. The words *quality, service,* and *cleanliness* were clearly less important than a growth strategy based on volume, cost control, and franchising. For example, McDonald's frozen burger patties are cooked using a special clamshell grill that cooks both sides of the patty at the same time. This is a remarkably fast and inexpensive way to cook burgers, but it may also be why McDonald's finished last in the 2010 Consumer Reports fast-food burger rankings.[5] (Yes, In-N-Out was rated number one.)

While franchising allowed McDonald's to grow into a global giant, it also made it difficult for the company to control the quality of service delivered at its restaurants. Today, approximately 80 percent of restaurants are run by franchisees and only 20 percent are corporate run by McDonald's,[6] which means the service that customers receive from most of its establishments is determined by the management skills and customer service philosophy of an independent franchise owner rather than by the McDonald's organization.

Of course, there are exceptions to every rule. Culture isn't exclusively defined by an entire organization. Even at McDonald's, restaurants with managers who are good at engaging employees and motivating them to deliver outstanding service typically bring in 10 percent more revenue per year than the average.[7]

In this chapter, we'll see how employees are influenced to conform to the organizational culture by their supervisor and their coworkers. We'll explore how company culture is ultimately a product of our actions rather than a catchy slogan or a set of corporate values. Along the way, we'll examine how a strong culture can be a major obstacle to outstanding customer service or a powerful force that lifts organizations to the ranks of the customer service elite.

Social Pressure Influences Behavior

Look at the pictures below. Which line (A, B, or C) is the same length as the one on the far left?

Psychologist Solomon Asch used cards with lines like these to conduct an experiment back in 1951. Subjects were told it was a visual acuity test, but it was really an experiment to see if people would conform to social pressure. In the experiment, a subject was placed in a room with several other people and asked to identify the matching line in a series of tests like this one. Unbeknownst to the subject, the other people in the room were actually Asch's assistants and had been instructed to give wrong answers.[8]

The subject was seated so that he'd be one of the last to respond. All of the participants gave their answers out loud, so each person could hear what the others had said. When the assistants all answered incorrectly, the subject also gave the wrong answer 36.8 percent of the time. Some subjects were more independent than others, but nearly 75 percent of them answered incorrectly at least once during the series of tests.[9]

Why did so many people give the wrong answer? Most subjects reported experiencing a conflict between what their eyes told them was the correct response and their desire to avoid contradicting the group. When debriefed after the experiment, the subjects provided a variety of rationales from "I am wrong, they are right" to "I didn't want to spoil the results of your experiment."

(The correct answer—as you probably identified—is C.)

Asch's experiment revealed that people tend to change their beliefs and actions out of a desire to conform to the norms of a larger group. In a customer service setting, these group norms are an important part of the company culture. Therefore, if the negative influence of the company culture is strong enough, an employee might knowingly provide poor customer service.

Here's a real-life example. Camille was a guest service associate in a hotel that struggled to serve its customers. She had the natural instincts to be good at customer service but found herself increasingly frustrated by her coworkers' apathetic attitudes toward guests. She soon found herself falling in line and delivering poor service herself. Giving less than her all in customer service situations bothered Camille, but her desire to avoid the discomfort of standing out from her coworkers was a stronger influence.

Camille eventually left this position to work as a guest-service associate in another hotel. Unlike at her last job, this hotel had a culture that valued customer service. Camille found encouragement through her coworkers, who all seemed to care deeply about doing their best to make guests happy.

She felt relieved that she could use her customer service skills without feeling like an outcast among her peers.

Organizational or group culture can even influence our behavior when we're not aware of it. In a 1935 experiment, psychologist Muzafer Sherif placed subjects in a darkened room and then turned on a tiny light at the far end of the room. In this situation, a phenomenon called the *autokinetic effect* causes us to perceive that the light is moving even though it's not. Subjects in the experiment, all unaware of the autokinetic effect, were asked to estimate how far the light moved.

Some subjects were placed in the room by themselves, and their estimates ranged from one-quarter to fifteen inches. Other subjects were seated in the room with two additional participants and asked to give their estimates aloud. This time, the group's estimates quickly converged to a group norm.

Sherif made two interesting discoveries about the groups in this experiment. First, most of the participants were unaware that the other members of the group had any influence on their perception of how far the light moved. They simply believed they were all giving reasonably accurate readings. Second, while there was consensus within the groups, the estimates varied widely between different groups.

These findings show that group norms readily influence our perceptions, yet how we're influenced depends on the dynamics of the particular group.[10] In a customer service setting, employees may not realize they are delivering mediocre or even poor service if they work in an environment where that is the norm. It may require moving to a new organization to realize there are other ways to serve.

Leslie manages an apartment community for a company that actively promotes a customer-focused culture. She often struggles to help new maintenance workers master the high level of customer service expected of all employees. Many of them come from other apartment communities where customer service was not a priority for this position.

Eventually, new employees begin to embrace customer service as a part of their job. They learn to prioritize repairs so that residents experience the least amount of inconvenience. The employees realize they are expected to engage residents in the community and provide them with assistance rather than simply pass them off to someone who works in the leasing office. Over time, they discover that they are expected to contribute ideas that will improve service.

Invariably, these employees give Leslie the same explanation for why customer service was so hard for them to master: "Every apartment community says service is important, but now I know that here you really mean it!"

Camille's and Leslie's experiences suggest that most employees aren't inherently good or bad at customer service. Their performance in any particular job can be hugely influenced by the culture that surrounds them. Lousy service might simply be a product of social pressure that encourages employees to treat customers poorly.

Negative social pressure often comes directly from supervisors. Not long ago, I noticed a declining service level at one of my favorite bakeries. The reason became clear when I heard the supervisor loudly chastising her employees for a missed order. As a customer, I was uncomfortable witnessing this tirade; I can only imagine how the employees felt as they were dressed down in front of several customers. There wasn't a smile to be seen on their faces as they went back to work.

This supervisor's rude approach created a great deal of negative pressure that caused her employees to perform poorly. They were clearly tentative in an effort to avoid her continued wrath, which made them less proactive and actually caused them to work slower. Her embarrassing public admonishment sent the message that it was okay to behave rudely in front of customers, and her employees quickly adopted a sullen attitude that was devoid of any enthusiasm.

Of course, negative social pressure can also come from coworkers. I once facilitated a workshop where the two most experienced employees were also the loudest detractors. Nothing I suggested met with their approval, and their negative outlook suppressed the other participants' willingness to participate in the training. Their supervisor was also attending the training, but he was too meek to stand up to these two curmudgeonly gentlemen.

We finally took a break to clear the air. When it was time to return, everyone made it back on time except for the two negative employees. The supervisor hesitantly asked the group members if they thought we should wait until they returned before restarting the class and was answered with a loud chorus of "No!" The rest of the class featured lively discussions and enthusiastic participation, and I breathed a sigh of relief when my two detractors never materialized.

Companies must simultaneously create positive social pressure while removing negative influences if they want their employees to provide outstanding service. Some of these solutions were covered in previous chapters, but here is a brief summary:

- Make time to catch employees providing good service and recognize their performance so that those employees will be likely to repeat it (see Chapter 3).

- Avoid policies that may anger customers and cause them to pressure your employees to perform poorly (see Chapter 4).

- Fix operational issues that contribute to customer service failures and frustrate employees (Chapter 5).

Another important way to create positive social pressure is for supervisors to act as role models for their employees. My first boss, Christie, was a master at reinforcing a positive customer service culture at the retail clothing store where I worked in high school. She spent a lot of time on the sales floor demonstrating the right way to treat customers through her own terrific example. She'd frequently spot associates doing something great and praise them for their efforts. Christie was also quick to get someone back on track if he didn't provide great service, though this didn't happen very often. She would even thank her employees for a great job at the end of each shift.

Christie's strong and consistent presence made it difficult for anyone to provide anything less than outstanding customer service. I always felt that I'd be letting her and my coworkers down if I didn't provide the best customer service I possibly could. The pressure to conform—in a good way—was always there.

One of the most difficult challenges for any supervisor is working with persistently negative employees. Left unchecked, they will attempt to spread their negative outlook to other people on the team. A supervisor must act decisively with these employees to help them adopt a more positive approach to customer service or remove them from the team.

A typical approach to managing employee performance is to pinpoint undesirable behaviors or results and get the employee to make a change. Consistently negative employees can be a real challenge to manage because gaining their agreement on what constitutes a bad attitude is usually difficult. Progressive discipline is also difficult to use in these situations because supervisors are often required to provide specific facts and examples when disciplining an employee.

When I was a young and inexperienced supervisor, I once sat down to counsel a veteran employee about her poor attitude. She responded by simply saying, "I don't have a bad attitude." I tried to back up my assertion with examples, but she countered each one by pointing out that she didn't believe she was being negative in those situations. I quickly realized I was over my head in this encounter.

Fortunately, I had access to a good mentor who was able to help me regroup and think about why I thought this employee had a bad attitude. My mentor encouraged me to look for objective data that was hard to refute. One of the key facts that emerged was that I had received five separate complaints from other department leaders who described my employee as difficult to work with.

I approached my employee once again and this time focused on the complaints. She didn't have to agree with her colleagues' impressions of her, I said, but it was important that she take steps to ensure the complaints didn't continue. Taking a more positive tone this time, I said I wanted to see her succeed and offered to brainstorm ways she might convince people in other departments that she was easy to work with.

The second conversation went very well. The feedback was a little difficult to take, but it was factual and, more important, actionable. My negative employee agreed to make changes, and over the course of the next few weeks, she succeeded in changing quite a few people's minds about her. Over time, she became a reliable employee who could work well with other departments.

Unfortunately, some employees simply refuse to change. In that case, customer service leaders need to act decisively to remove those individuals from the team. Losing a disgruntled employee can be like a breath of fresh air and reinvigorate the rest of the team. On the other hand, letting a negative employee stay too long can cause others to yield to that person's influence, with the team in general losing respect for the supervisor's authority.

Culture Is What We Do

Jim Collins investigated the traits of enduring companies in his book *Built to Last*. Companies that succeeded over a long period of time, he discovered, built "cult-like" cultures. Their culture was deliberately ingrained in everything they did and continually reinforced at all levels of the organization.[11]

When you look at the companies most admired for their customer service, you'll discover that every one of them has a clearly defined culture that focuses everyone in the organization on serving customers. Many of these companies are profiled in books and magazine articles. Some, like

Disney, share their culture-building secrets through corporate training programs.

If a customer-focused culture is so important, and information on how to create one is so widely available, why don't more companies have one? The short answer is that creating a customer-focused culture takes real dedication. Companies that just go through the motions tend to fall short.

Some companies hire ad agencies to develop clever marketing messages that highlight outstanding customer experiences. Defunct electronics retailer Circuit City was once famous for its slogan, "Welcome to Circuit City, where service is state of the art." But service was definitely not state of the art when Circuit City filed for bankruptcy in 2008. That year, its customer service was ranked second to last for specialty retail stores by the American Customer Satisfaction Index.[12] Ironically, Circuit City's undoing was related to strategic decisions made over many years that resulted in poor customer service. For example, the company implemented a 15 percent restocking fee on returned products. The decision to impose this fee stemmed from a belief that many customers wanted to buy items, use them, and then return them for a refund. But the fee was widely criticized and even underwent legal scrutiny.[13] In another highly publicized example, Circuit City fired thousands of its most experienced and knowledgeable retail associates and replaced them with less-expensive (and less-experienced) employees. This decision saved the company some money in the short term, but it also sent the message that the company regarded employees as commodities rather than a source of competitive advantage. Clearly, the customer didn't come first when making this move.[14]

Some companies think it's enough to create lofty customer service platitudes at executive retreats. One company spent a great deal of time and money creating a set of five customer service values that it rolled out to all employees. The company hired me to determine how well the employees understood the new values.

I started by surveying employees throughout the company to test their recollection of the customer service values. A huge majority (95 percent) of the employees could recite all five values from memory. The remaining 5 percent got four out of five correct. So far, so good.

Next, I asked employees to tell me what the values meant. Here, there was near-universal disagreement. Even the CEO, the CFO, and the vice president of operations had different definitions! They'd spent so much time coming up with the perfect words that they hadn't stopped to ensure they all understood the same meaning.

Finally, I asked employees how the five customer service values influenced their daily activities. Quite a few believed the service values were a slogan that didn't reflect their true culture. Even more disturbing was a widespread belief that the company's executives failed to consistently align their own decisions and actions with the values. The feeling among many employees was, "Our CEO doesn't really believe in these customer service values, so why should I?"

Some companies have tried to institutionalize a customer-focused culture by including it in formal training programs or an orientation video. This is an admirable step, but two factors can quickly cancel it out if there's no real commitment.

First, the institutional culture message is often delivered by someone other than an employee's direct supervisor. New hires learn about company culture in new employee orientation, during a special training class delivered by a corporate trainer, or perhaps they are shown a slick video created by the marketing department. However, the employee's supervisor needs to understand and believe in the company culture, too. If the supervisor doesn't model the same message, the employee will almost always follow the supervisor's lead, since the boss has direct control over the employee's performance.

Second, most of what employees learn does not come from formal training. The American Society for Training and Development (ASTD) estimates that 70 percent or more of workplace learning is informal.[15] This informal learning includes on-the-job training, sharing with coworkers, taking direction from supervisors, reading policies and procedures, and learning from experience. If there's a conflict between the cultural message delivered in formal training and the cultural message learned informally, the latter will almost always win.

Developing a strong customer-focused culture requires an ongoing commitment and dedication, but organizations repeatedly try to find shortcuts that ultimately result in failure. They hold team-building events or hire someone like me to deliver a motivational speech to get everyone fired up about service. Unfortunately, these high-energy events often represent the extent of the initiative.

A client of mine once hired me to deliver a keynote address on creating a customer service culture. My presentation was part of a four-day leadership conference where the focus was using customer service to set the company apart from the competition and drive sales. By the time I took the stage the energy from the group of leaders was unbelievable. They cheered and applauded each other. Whenever someone gave the signal, everyone would stand and loudly chant the new customer service principles. It was as if they were at a giant pep rally before a big game. They even had noisemakers and confetti to throw around the room that contributed to the festive atmosphere.

Inevitably, these leaders had to come back down to earth after their conference. When reality set in and they went back to their locations, they were confronted with a mountain of new tasks, initiatives, and directives. All of this new work and the steady pull of ingrained habits did more to shape their performance than any good intentions they took away from the leadership conference. Sadly, the company announced massive layoffs a few months later when it was unable to meet its service or profit goals.

Culture is what we actually do. It can't be created by a marketing campaign, a vision statement, a training program, or a motivational conference. Creating a customer-focused culture takes time, commitment, and perseverance. Most important, it's a never-ending process.

The first step in creating a customer-focused culture is to clearly define it. You must give employees clear direction so that they know how they can contribute. Here are the three hallmarks of a clear definition of customer-focused culture:

1. The definition is simple and easily understood.

2. It describes the type of service we want to achieve for our customers.

3. It reflects both who we are now and who we aspire to be in the future.

In-N-Out Burger is a great example of a company with a clearly defined customer service philosophy written in plain English:

> Give customers the freshest, highest quality foods you can buy and provide them with friendly service in a sparkling clean environment.[16]

This philosophy is immediately apparent when you walk into any In-N-Out restaurant. Look into the open kitchen, and you'll see fresh produce or an employee using a slicer to cut whole potatoes into fries. You'll be greeted by a cheerful employee who makes eye contact, smiles, and thanks you sincerely. You'll notice how clean the restaurant is, even if you happen to stop in during a busy time when the dining area is full of customers. Finally, your experience all comes together when you sit down and take a bite of one of their delicious cheeseburgers.

The second step in creating a customer-focused culture is setting goals that represent forward progress toward the company's definition of outstanding service. A good customer service goal isn't something you write and then tuck away in a drawer somewhere. It must be continually reviewed and discussed so that employees know how they're doing and can take action to keep making progress.

Customer service goals must have three qualities to effectively encourage positive performance:

1. The goal should focus employees on the desired performance, rather than divert their attention away from the big picture.

2. The goal should encourage cooperation by emphasizing team achievement rather than individual outcomes.

3. The goal should tap into employees' intrinsic motivation, rather than rely on external rewards to drive performance.

Starwood Hotels is an organization that effectively uses goals to drive outstanding service. Like most hotels, Starwood regularly captures guest feedback through surveys. The survey scores are combined into a Guest Service Index, or GSI score, that's an important indicator of hotel performance.

The Westin Portland, one of Starwood's locations, provides a glimpse into how goals can drive behavior. Every associate at the Westin Portland understands that guest satisfaction is a top priority. Associates review their GSI scores on a daily basis and obsess about the results. They talk about their results in team meetings, share stories, and ask each other for feedback.

Teamwork is essential to the Westin Portland's never-ending quest for guest satisfaction. Associates coach and encourage each other to deliver high levels of service that will help them achieve their GSI goals. Departments hold friendly contests to see who can get the best GSI results. The hotel's leadership team regularly discusses guest feedback with the associates and encourages people to share ideas that will improve service even further.

What they don't do is offer incentives to achieve their GSI goals. The hotel's former general manager, Chris Lorino, instilled a philosophy that achieving the highest possible GSI score should be viewed as a primary responsibility for every associate. He felt that implementing an incentive program would divert the associates' focus to earning the incentive rather than pleasing guests. Chris has since been promoted, in part because of the outstanding service his team achieved, but the Westin Portland continues to rely on its associates' innate desire to deliver the best possible service.

The third step toward creating a customer-focused culture is for leaders and managers to recognize and act upon the "moments of truth" that truly define a culture. A moment of truth refers to the myriad of daily decisions a customer service leader must make. These decisions include hiring, training, policy making, budgeting, and supervising. A company can claim to have a truly customer-focused culture only when the vast majority of its leaders' decisions align with the company's definition of outstanding service.

My local plumbing company is an example of an organization that has developed a reputation for outstanding service by mastering the moments of truth. Plumbers generally have a reputation of showing up late, creating a big mess, and charging enormous fees. Ideal Plumbing, Heating, Air, and Electrical does the opposite by making customer service a priority in everything its employees do.

For Don Teemsma, Ideal's president, the hiring process represents the first moment of truth. According to Don, every technician the company hires must have both outstanding technical and customer service skills. Each candidate is carefully screened and interviewed by at least one manager and one coworker, and any interviewer has the authority to reject a candidate if the interviewer believes the person wouldn't live up to Ideal's high standards.

Hiring great people is just the beginning for Ideal. Don and his management team consistently reinforce their customer service philosophy through training, regular team meetings, and daily one-on-one interaction with employees. Don spends a good part of each day checking in on customers at the job site or over the phone, to make sure things are going smoothly. From a customer's perspective, Ideal's consistent focus on these "moments of truth" results in an extraordinarily high level of service.

Solution Summary: Creating a Customer-Focused Culture

Employees are powerfully influenced by their workplace culture. Delivering outstanding service requires organizations to develop a positive, customer-focused culture—but it also takes more hard work, discipline, and dedication than many organizations realize. Here is a summary of the solutions discussed in this chapter:

- Ensure that your customer service leaders act as role models who actively demonstrate a positive customer-focused attitude and encourage their employees to do the same.

- Work closely with persistently negative employees to help them change their behavior, or else remove them from the team if they are unwilling or unable to do so. These employees can be detrimental to both customer service and team morale if their behavior is left unchecked.

- Create a clear definition of your customer service philosophy so that employees receive clear direction and can easily understand how they can contribute.

- Develop customer service goals that help motivate employees and keep them focused on providing the highest level of service possible.

- Win the moments of truth that define an organization's true culture.

Notes

1. Raymund Flandez, "In-N-Out Burger vs. McDonald's: Guess Who Won?" Independent Street (blog), *Wall Street Journal*, January 28, 2009.

2. McDonald's was ranked last in the 2010 American Customer Satisfaction Index (www.theacsi. org) for limited service restaurants. In-N-Out is a regional restaurant chain and was not included in this study.

3. You can read more about each company's history on their respective websites: www.in-n-out. com and www.aboutmcdonalds.com.

4. Stacy Perman, *In-N-Out Burger: A Behind-the-Counter Look at the Fast-Food Chain That Breaks All the Rules* (New York, Collins Business, 2009).

5. "Our readers reveal: Best Burgers," *Consumer Reports*, October 2010.

6. McDonald's Corporation 2010 Annual Report.

7. Lauren Young, "McDonald's Supersized Retirement Plan," *Businessweek*, January 12, 2009.

8. S. E. Asch, "Opinions and social pressure," *Scientific American* 193, no. 5 (1955), pp. 31–35.

9. Kendra Cherry, "The Asch Conformity Experiments," *About Psychology*, http://psychology. about.com/od/classicpsychologystudies/p/conformity.htm.

10. Muzafer Sherif, "A Study of Some Social Factors in Perception," *Archives of Psychology* 27, no. 187 (1935).

11. Jim Collins and Jerry I. Porras, *Built to Last: Successful Habits of Visionary Companies* (New York: HarperCollins, 1994).

12. The American Customer Satisfaction Index, 2008 Specialty Retail Stores Results www.theacsi.org

13. Thomas J. Lueck, "Consumer Chief Lambastes Circuit City Return Policy," *New York Times*, December 27, 1997.

14. Anita Hamilton, "Why Circuit City Busted, While Best Buy Boomed," *Time*, November 11, 2008; www.time.com/time/business/article/0,8599,1858079,00.html.

15. "Tapping the Potential of Informal Learning: An ASTD Research Study." American Society for Training & Development whitepaper, 2008. Available at www.astd.org

16. From In-N-Out Burger's corporate employment website, www.in-n-out.com/employment/corporate.aspx.

CHAPTER 7

Attention Is in Short Supply

Getting Employees to Notice What Customers Really Need

My wife, Sally, and I flew into San Francisco for a getaway weekend and arrived at our hotel before check-in time. Hotels will often let you check in early if the room is ready, but the front desk agent informed us that our room wouldn't be available for another forty-five minutes. We told her we'd relax in the lobby, and she assured us she'd let us know as soon as our room was ready. There were some overstuffed chairs directly in front of the check-in counter that looked comfortable, so we grabbed a seat and settled in for the wait.

I'm fascinated by observing people provide customer service, so I passed the time by watching the front desk agent and her coworkers. They seemed engaged in a never-ending flurry of activity. A steady stream of people approached the counter to check in or out, ask for directions, or make some other request. The phones rang frequently, and our front desk agent had to pause to answer. She also seemed to have quite a bit of computer work to do, since she filled the time between guests and phone calls by working away at the keyboard in front of her.

Sally and I started to get a little anxious as we neared the forty-five-minute mark, since it was a beautiful day and we were eager to go explore the city. We both started watching the front desk agent in anticipation that any minute now she'd wave us over and let us know our room was ready. She was such a whirlwind of activity that we assumed she was on top of it.

But forty-five minutes soon became an hour, with no sign from the hotel associate. We finally went back to the counter and asked for an update. She took a moment to look us up on her computer and said, "You can check in now, your room has been ready for half an hour."

She had forgotten us! We were literally sitting in front of her for an hour, and she had forgotten we were there. Even worse, we could have checked in thirty minutes earlier. She didn't even apologize.

Situations like this occur every day in customer service. From a customer's perspective, it couldn't be more obvious. The employee simply needs to pay more attention.

In this chapter, we'll see that one of the challenges to providing outstanding customer service is that our attention is in increasingly short supply. In some cases, employees' attention is divided among too many tasks, which can cause employees to miss opportunities to serve. At other times, employees can become so focused on one thing that they develop tunnel vision and again miss important cues from their customers. We'll even discover a way that our brain naturally causes us to stop listening by jumping to conclusions. None of these obstacles are insurmountable, but companies need to provide customer service representatives with a lot of training and assistance to help them pay careful attention to their customers' needs.

The Curse of Multitasking

As I write this chapter, there are more than a thousand customer service jobs advertised on the website Monster.com listing "multitasking" in the job description. There's even a posting for a medical billing specialist with "outstanding customer service abilities and sixth sense instincts." I imagine "sixth sense" is intended figuratively, since companies wouldn't seriously require job applicants to have some sort of ESP. However, companies would do well to look at multitasking in the same light as having a sixth sense.

Multitasking, the way most people define it, isn't possible because the human brain is capable of handling only one conscious thought at a time. According to studies conducted by David Meyer, a researcher at the University of Michigan's Brain Cognition and Action Laboratory, when we attempt to multitask, our brain is actually rapidly switching between the various tasks we're trying to attend to. A little bit of time is lost whenever we move from one task to the next because our brain must refocus.[1]

The only situation where we can effectively perform more than one task at a time is when just one of those tasks requires conscious attention. That's why we're able to carry on a conversation with someone over the phone while we doodle on a notepad, but we aren't very good at having that same conversation while trying to send someone else an e-mail.

To illustrate the challenges with multitasking, there's a test known as the Stroop effect, named after an experiment conducted in 1935 by the American psychologist John Ridley Stroop. In the experiment, subjects were shown a series of squares and asked to identify the color of each one as quickly as possible. Subjects were then shown a list of words that were the names of a color. The words were all printed in colored ink, and subjects were asked to identify the color each word was printed in as quickly as possible. The catch was that the word and the color the word was printed in didn't match, so the word *red* may have been printed in blue ink while *orange* may have been printed in green. On average, subjects took 74 percent longer to identify all the colors in this second list where the color of the ink didn't match the word.[2] (You can try a Stroop test yourself here: http://faculty.washington.edu/chudler/java/ready.html.)

In a service environment, our inability to multitask means employees must either choose between two conscious tasks or do both with far less efficiency. Think back to a time when you were served by someone who was speaking to another customer on the phone. One of two things probably happened. The first possibility was that the customer service rep asked you to wait or put the caller on hold so that she could serve one person at a time. The second possibility was that the rep tried to serve you while speaking to the other person, which resulted in her paying substantially less attention to you.

Our inability to effectively focus on two things at once isn't the only challenge employees face when it comes to multitasking. Today's modern work environment is full of auditory and visual stimuli that constantly vie for our attention. The way our brain interacts with these attention-catching stimuli naturally encourages people to switch rapidly between tasks.

Attention is captured in two primary ways. The first is known as "top-down" attention, where we consciously focus on a particular goal or task. The second is known as "bottom-up," or stimulus-driven, attention, where an external stimulus grabs our attention, such as a phone ringing or a person suddenly standing in front of us.[3]

Our top-down attention can override our bottom-up attention, allowing us to tune out external distractions, but it requires deliberate concentration. However, the more our attention is captured by external bottom-up stimuli, the harder it is for our brain to consciously refocus its attention on a specific goal. The inevitable result of too many distractions is that we find it hard to concentrate and complete a single task that we might be able to quickly accomplish if there weren't so many other things competing for our attention.[4]

Now let's think back to the hotel's front desk associate. She was bombarded by external stimuli. The phones were ringing, coworkers interrupted her, and guests continually approached her. The conflict between her top-down goal of completing certain responsibilities (e.g., letting us know when our room was ready) and the bottom-up attention grabbers (e.g., someone interrupting her to ask a question) caused her to constantly switch tasks. Each time this happened, my wife and I were pushed farther and farther away from her conscious mind until we eventually disappeared completely.

Many customer service employees are continuously interrupted by external stimuli that naturally encourage them to multitask. A server in a busy restaurant must keep tabs on multiple tables while being interrupted by guests. A retail cashier must try to ring up customer transactions while other customers interrupt to ask questions. Even someone working in an office environment is subjected to frequent interruptions by coworkers, new e-mail messages flashing onto the computer screen, and even that catchy song on the radio.

Some people argue that multitasking really refers to the ability to manage multiple priorities. By the dictionary definition, a priority is something that merits attention ahead of competing alternatives. This concept often invites confusion and poor performance when customer service priorities are not clearly identified and an employee is unable to consciously choose between tasks based upon their level of importance. When I take my car in for service, I typically spend a moment at the service counter with a customer service representative going over the repair bill. The phone will frequently ring while we are having our conversation, which brings us to a customer service dilemma.

The ringing phone is an external attention grabber that the customer service rep is certain to notice. The rep must now choose between continuing our conversation or interrupting it to answer the phone. She can't do both, so one task must become more important than the other.

Her choice depends on her priorities. The rep will continue serving me if the priority is finishing up with the customer she's already working with. However, she will interrupt our conversation and answer the phone if the priority is making sure all calls are answered within a certain number of rings.

What will happen if the priorities aren't clearly defined? The rep will answer the phone. Without a specific intention to consciously focus on one task over another, the ringing phone will capture the employee's attention and the natural inclination will be to answer it. After finishing the phone conversation or putting the caller on hold, the customer service representative will come back to me and say, "Now, where were we?"

With all the interruptions in the workplace, our natural inclination to focus on external stimuli, and a lack of clear priorities, it's no wonder that customer service representatives find it difficult to be fully engaged with the task at hand. Their attention is constantly being pulled in any number of directions, which causes them to work less efficiently, make more errors, and ultimately provide their customers with poor treatment. Companies must help their employees do a better job of focusing their attention on customers if they want to deliver outstanding service.

The best way to help employees pay the right amount of attention to the right things at the right time is to make it easier for them to work within their natural abilities. This means creating a work environment where employees are able to focus on priorities and ignore distractions.

The first step employers should take is to discourage employees from performing more than one conscious task at a time. I once used this concept to help a client improve order-entry productivity and accuracy in their contact center. The company's customer service representatives were responsible for retrieving orders faxed in by clients and entering them into the computer in between customer calls.

The data entry seemed like a great way to fill the time between each call, but it also led to some unintended consequences. The phone often rang while reps were halfway through entering an order, so they had to hurriedly save the order while switching their focus to the person on the phone. Some reps would try to cheat a little and complete the task they were working on while they answered the call, but this often caused them to give a poor greeting, or even miss the reason for the person's call. The start-and-stop nature of the data entry clearly caused diminished productivity and high error rates.

You may have guessed by now that the simple solution was dividing responsibilities. A handful of reps were taken off the phones entirely so that they could focus attention on entering orders received via fax. Their productivity immediately soared and their error rates dropped because they could work at a constant pace without interruption. With fewer reps taking calls, the reps on the phones had less downtime to try to squeeze in additional tasks and were able to fully devote their attention to customers on the phone.

Another way companies can help employees pay attention to the right thing is through the use of automatic reminders, which are helpful auditory or visual alerts that capture someone's attention at just the right time. The alarm on your calendar or cell phone reminds you to head to a meeting. Baristas at coffee shops use little timers to remind them to check on the brewing coffee. Call center representatives often have little windows that pop up on their computer screen to remind them to make a special offer or provide their customers with certain information.

Why automatic? Automatic reminders are simply more reliable than our own memories or even relying on other people. When we think back to the front desk associate who forgot to tell us that our room was ready, we can see it's very possible she thought she would remember to check on us, without realizing just how soon she would be consumed with other work. Or she might have been relying on a phone call from someone in housekeeping to let her know the room was ready, but that system would fail if the housekeeper forgot to call. Relying on your frazzled memory or on other, equally harried people to remind you to do something is, unfortunately, a recipe for forgetfulness.

A third way for companies to help their employees is to firmly establish customer service priorities. If you recall, employees may have a difficult time paying attention to the right tasks when they face confusing or competing priorities. Clear priorities that are frequently communicated and consistently followed can help employees make the right choices in situations where there are competing tasks.

The Walt Disney Company sets clear priorities for its cast members (Disney's term for employees) so that they will know what's important in any given situation. I once saw it in action while riding the Twilight

Zone Tower of Terror, a thrill ride that simulates being stuck in a runaway elevator inside a haunted hotel. Everyone had just belted into his or her seat when a young boy started crying and protesting that he didn't want to go on the scary ride. The cast member playing the "demented elevator operator" immediately broke out of his character and invited the boy to step off the ride. He assured the boy's concerned mother that he would keep a close eye on her son while she enjoyed the ride. When we returned and the elevator doors opened, the cast member was waiting with the now-smiling boy standing next to him.

Disney's priorities clearly guided the cast member's actions. Safety is the first priority, as evidenced by his delaying the ride and making sure the boy safely exited. The second priority is courtesy, so the cast member momentarily paused his scripted routine to politely address the young boy and assure the mother that her son would be safe. The show is Disney's third priority, so the cast member quickly resumed his act once the first two priorities were addressed.[5]

Paying TOO Much Attention Isn't a Good Idea, Either

Customer service representatives are often guilty of not paying enough attention, but paying too much attention to a single customer or task can have consequences, too. Here's an example.

I was dining at one of my favorite local restaurants with my wife and her parents. We received lousy service throughout our meal and hardly saw our server after she took our orders. Our water glasses sat empty and we finished our food before she came back to take our drink order. It even took a long time just to get our check.

Why was our service so poor? The most likely explanation was that our server was paying too much attention to a large group seated in the middle of her section. The members of this party arrived in a steady stream rather than all at once, so she was constantly going back to them to take a new drink or food order. Large groups can be difficult for servers to handle, and we could clearly see that she was focusing her attention on making sure these people were happy.

Paying so much attention to the large group caused her to develop tunnel vision, which made it difficult for her to see us or remember our needs. She repeatedly walked within eyesight of our table on her way to the kitchen without even glancing in our direction. We even resorted to waving at her in an attempt to capture her attention, but she seemed completely absorbed with taking care of this large party.

Our poor service may have been attributable to something called *inattentional blindness*. Think of it as the opposite of the front desk associate who was constantly distracted. It's possible to be so focused on a specific task that you tune out external stimuli that would otherwise be very obvious.

An amazing experiment conducted by Christopher Chabris and Daniel Simons illustrates this effect. (You may want to try it yourself before reading further by watching this short video on YouTube at http://youtube/vJG698U2Mvo.)

In the experiment, subjects are asked to watch a short video that features two teams of three people. One team is wearing white T-shirts while the other team is dressed in black T-shirts. Both teams are passing basketballs back and forth among their teammates while mingling with members of the other team. The subjects in the experiment were asked to watch the video and count the number of times the team in white passes the basketball.

About halfway through the video, a person dressed in a gorilla suit walks into view from the right side of the screen. The gorilla slowly walks through the two teams passing their basketballs, coming to a stop in the middle of the scene. It faces the camera and pounds its chest before turning to its right and slowly walking off screen.

Amazingly, Chabris and Simons discovered that nearly 50 percent of the test subjects failed to notice the person in the gorilla costume. The test subjects who missed the gorilla were so focused on counting the white team's basketball passes that they tuned everything else out, including the gorilla![6]

There are many situations where inattentional blindness, or "invisible gorillas," may lead to poor customer service. A grocery store cashier discussing her break schedule with her supervisor may miss a chance to greet the customer standing in front of her. A retail associate consumed with folding a stack of sweaters may not notice a customer who clearly needs help finding a pair of jeans. A customer service representative may get so focused on clearing out a slew of e-mails that he hardly bothers to read each one before pasting in a stock reply and hitting Send.

The challenge of inattentional blindness can be compounded by a belief that an employee should have seen something so obvious. If Chabris and Simons hadn't documented their experiment, who would believe that so many people wouldn't notice a gorilla calmly strolling through a short video? Likewise, customer service supervisors often chalk up episodes of inattentional blindness to an employee's carelessness. A restaurant manager might tell a server, "You need to pay more attention," without understanding the real reason that she repeatedly ignored several of her tables while attending to the needs of a large group.

Inattentional blindness may be another reason my wife and I became invisible to the hotel's front desk associate. There were several occasions when she wasn't being interrupted by a phone call, another guest, or a coworker. During those times, she turned her attention to her computer and intently focused on her stack of paperwork. The concentration required to complete those computer tasks may have caused her to deliberately tune out any additional stimuli, such as two guests patiently waiting in the lobby right in front of her.

There are a couple of ways to help employees avoid inattentional blindness. The first is to reduce the amount of tasks employees are expected to accomplish in addition to serving customers. Tasks tend to take employees' focus away from helping people because supervisors can easily observe whether a task is completed while customer interactions are usually harder to monitor.

Home Depot has used this strategy to dramatically improve its customer service levels. Since 2007, Home Depot's customer service ratings have risen steadily after hitting rock bottom with a 67 percent satisfaction score on the American Customer Satisfaction Index.[7] A core component of the company's turnaround was reducing the number of tasks assigned to sales associates and putting more people on the floor, making it easier for customers to get assistance. This approach even extended to store management teams, where more than 200 weekly reports and e-mails were eliminated in favor of a simple one-page scorecard.[8] Just three years later, Home Depot's customer satisfaction rating had risen to 75 percent.

Another way to avoid inattentional blindness is to create the expectation that employees proactively greet any customer who comes near them. In hospitality industries, where employees have face-to-face customer contact, this technique is referred to as the 10 & 5 Rule: Associates are expected to give any guest within ten feet a nonverbal acknowledgment, such as a smile or a wave, and verbally greet any guest who is within five feet. In retail, it's known as "zone coverage," where associates are expected to greet any customer who comes into their department or assigned part of the store. Employees can avoid inattentional blindness by continually scanning for customers in need of assistance rather than waiting for customers to approach them.

Listening to Customers Can Be Difficult

So far in this chapter, we've examined obstacles that keep employees from focusing on their customers. When a customer does manage to capture an employee's attention, it may still be difficult for the employee to truly listen. Our own brain can sometimes be the source of distractions that prevent us from understanding our customers' needs.

Time pressure is one example. When people feel rushed or hurried, they may find their mind wandering in anticipation of the next task. Seeing a long line can cause a cashier to work a little faster and pay a little less attention to each individual customer in an effort to keep the line moving. Call centers often have large display boards that indicate the number of callers on hold, along with their average wait time, which can encourage reps to hurry through calls when those numbers get beyond acceptable limits. Even employees who handle e-mail correspondence can miss important pieces of their customers' messages when they are working too fast to clear a backlog of inquiries.

Yet another obstacle is that, even when we're consciously focused on a particular task, our brain can sometimes override our concentration by jumping to conclusions. I once experienced a classic example of this phenomenon when I called a customer service number to get some help with a password for accessing my online account. I was halfway through my question when the customer service representative interrupted me and said, "That's actually a separate password than the one I'm resetting for you. That one is just for billing."

Great, except that wasn't the question I was about to ask. "I know," I said, "but I was going to ask if I can reset the billing password myself so that I . . ."

He interrupted again: "But you don't need the billing password to access your online account." *Sigh.* Still not the question I was trying to ask.

Why do so many knowledgeable customer service representatives find it difficult to listen to their customers without interrupting? This problem is related to how we naturally process information.

The human brain has a unique design feature that allows us to take a small amount of information and compare it to familiar patterns. This capability allows us to make quick sense of large amounts of data without getting bogged down in the details. It's an ability that comes in handy in many ways, such as determining if something is safe or dangerous, recognizing people we know, or even when reading.

Here's a simple example. Try reading the sentence below:

People can easliy raed misspleled wrods as long as all the lettres are there and the fisrt and lsat letters are in the corerct position.

Thanks to our handy pattern-recognition ability, you can read sentences like this one and understand them. Your brain recognizes the pattern presented by the arrangement of the letters and the context of the sentence. It doesn't matter that the letters aren't perfectly placed; they're close enough for your brain to quickly understand the meaning.[9]

It's this same ability that can get customer service representatives into trouble when it comes to listening. The customer service representative I talked to about resetting my billing password had undoubtedly heard questions similar to mine many times. The start of my sentence fit a familiar pattern, so his brain stopped listening and presented an answer to the question he thought I was going to ask. The problem occurred because my question was a new variation on this familiar pattern, so the answer that leaped into his mind was incorrect.

Effective listening skills are often taken for granted; as a result, many employees are given little support or training in this area. Employees themselves can overestimate their own abilities because they often receive some of their customer's message and mistakenly believe they heard all of their customer's needs. Companies that want to deliver outstanding customer service must offer training and coaching to help their employees become better listeners.

Training customer service employees on active listening skills is a good place to start. Active listening requires us to be fully engaged with the person we are listening to. To be an active listener you should physically face the speaker, make eye contact, and provide nonverbal cues that indicate the other person has your attention, such as nodding. Employees should learn to ask clarifying questions and to paraphrase what their customer is saying to confirm understanding. Most important, employees must develop the ability to consciously suspend judgment until they are certain they understand what their customer is asking for. These skills allow customer service reps to focus on their customer, making it easier to tune out distractions and resist the urge to jump to conclusions.

Regular coaching and feedback will help customer service reps to keep their listening skills sharp. Constructive feedback can illuminate the blind spots that we can all develop, such as the habit of trying to finish the other person's sentences. Supervisors should regularly observe customer interactions and help their employees identify opportunities for continual improvement.

Finally, reduce time pressure whenever possible by providing adequate staffing levels so that employees can work efficiently without being pressured to compromise service quality. Tight budgets can make it tempting for customer service leaders to cut back on staffing, but this decision may result in increased customer complaints and, ultimately, reduced revenue as dissatisfied customers take their business elsewhere. In Chapter 11, we'll examine this issue in greater detail.

Solution Summary: Helping Employees Pay Better Attention

Customer service should be priority number one for customer service employees, but as we've learned, actions speak louder than words. Employees often need help to pay careful attention to each customer. Here is a summary of the solutions discussed in this chapter:

- Develop work processes and procedures that discourage employees from trying to complete more than one task at a time.

- Create automatic reminders that capture employees' attention at the right moment such as a pop-up screen that reminds an employee to return a customer's call.

- Establish and reinforce clear customer service priorities so that employees know where to focus their attention.

- Reduce the number of tasks that customer service employees are expected to complete, so they can devote more attention to serving customers.

- Help employees put customers first by maintaining an expectation that they proactively greet anyone who is in their vicinity.

- Train employees to use active listening skills when serving customers.

- Provide appropriate staffing levels so employees aren't tempted to compromise service quality in an effort to serve more people.

Notes

1. David Meyer's website offers a very good introductory explanation of multitasking, as well as several research papers; see www.umich.edu/~bcalab/multitasking.html.

2. J. Ridley Stroop, "Studies of Interference in Serial Verbal Reactions," *Journal of Experimental Psychology* 18 (1935), pp. 643–662.

3. Steven L. Franconeri, Justin A. Junge, and Daniel J. Simons, "Searching for Stimulus-Driven Shifts of Attention," *Psychonomic Bulletin & Review* 11, no. 5 (October 2004), pp. 876–881.

4. Valerio Santangelo, Marta Olivetti Belardinelli, Charles Spence, and Emiliano Macaluso, "Interactions Between Voluntary and Stimulus-Driven Spatial Attention Mechanisms Across Sensory Modalities," *Journal of Cognitive Neuroscience* 21, no. 12 (December 2009), pp. 2384–2397.

5. Ted Topping, "Day Two: Disney's Service Values," *DisneyDispatch.com*, April 28, 2011.

6. Christopher Chabris and Daniel Simons, *The Invisible Gorilla and Other Ways Our Intuitions Deceive Us* (New York: Crown Publishing, 2010).

7. The American Customer Satisfaction Index, Specialty Retail Stores, www.theacsi.org/index.php?option=com_content&view=category&id=18.

8. Patricia O'Connell, "Putting the Customer FIRST at Home Depot," *Bloomberg Businessweek,* November 5, 2010.

9. It's a great service to the world when people like Matt Davis of the Medical Research Council (MRC) Cognition and Brain Sciences Unit at the University of Cambridge take the time to summarize a heap of research in one coherent paper. You'll also learn that my misspelled sentence is not 100 percent accurate. See http://www.mrc-cbu.cam.ac.uk/people/matt.davis/Cmabrigde/.

CHAPTER 8

What Role Will You Play Today?

Emphasizing the Primary Responsibility to Delight Customers

I played many roles when I was a teenager working in a local clothing store.

On most days, I focused on delivering outstanding customer service by greeting every customer who came into my department and using my product knowledge to help customers find the perfect outfits in the right size. I tried to project a fun, upbeat attitude to help make customers' shopping experiences pleasant and easy.

Sometimes I played the role of cashier. I still tried to deliver terrific customer service, but my focus was narrower. There was a steady stream of customers paying for their purchases on busy days, so I worked hard to be both pleasant and efficient. On slower days, I ventured away from the cash register to tidy up merchandise in the immediate area, but I didn't wander too far so that I wouldn't miss someone who was ready to be rung up.

Once a week my role was stocking the latest deliveries of jeans. I stationed myself on the sales floor with a box of them, removing each pair from the box, attaching an alarm tag, folding them, and organizing them according to size on our display. I still assisted customers, but I was less proactive about service because my main goal was to empty out as many boxes of jeans as I could before the end of my shift.

A couple of times each week, I worked a closing shift. When we worked closing, we couldn't go home for the evening until the entire store had been vacuumed and all the clothes straightened and put away. The dressing rooms had to be cleaned, too, and the trash taken out. Nobody wanted to stay late, so we would cheat a little and start cleaning up about an hour before closing time. Customers who came in a few minutes before closing were unlikely to get much help since we were preoccupied with cleaning.

Occasionally my role focused on theft prevention. I'd been trained to spot potential shoplifters and was expected to follow them around the store. Some people quickly left when they realized they were being watched, some turned out to be great customers who made large purchases, and others simply got annoyed when they realized they were being followed. Ironically, the term for hassling potential thieves was "customer servicing."

In this chapter, we'll examine the strong connection between the level of customer service employees provide and their understanding of the role they are playing. We'll see how employees often define their role in terms of the tasks they are asked to complete rather than the assistance their customers want. We'll also learn how, in some extreme cases, otherwise good people can find themselves treating their customers horribly due to a twisted sense of their responsibilities or blind obedience to an unethical or uncaring boss. Companies that wish to deliver outstanding customer service must ensure their employees know their ultimate responsibility is serving the customer.

When Tasks Define Our Roles

Many customer service employees I speak with define their roles by the tasks they perform. If they're cashiers, they say, "I ring up purchases."

If they work in technical support, they say, "I fix computers." If they're receptionists, they say, "I greet visitors."

But these descriptions don't describe *how* these employees should actually be helping their customers. Customers want cashiers to make paying for purchases a fast and hassle-free experience. Customers want technical support reps to help them minimize the lost productivity and aggravation that comes with a malfunctioning computer. Customers want receptionists to make them feel welcome and connect them with the person they came to visit.

This task focus is often the cause of poor customer service because the ultimate goal of delighting customers fades into the background. Let's say you order a new cell phone online, but the company sends the wrong model. You follow the directions on the packing slip and call the customer service department for a return authorization number so that you can return the phone and get the one you ordered. In that moment, you're feeling disappointed that you can't use your new cell phone, annoyed that you have to go through the hassle of returning the one they sent, and frustrated because the company requires you to jump through hoops before it will fix its mistake and send the correct one.

What's the customer service representative's role in this situation? The focus should be on turning around a disappointing, annoying, and frustrating experience. Unfortunately, task-oriented employees are likely to think their primary goal is to issue the return authorization number so that they can quickly move on to the next call. The length of their call might even be closely measured, giving them an extra incentive to get you off the phone quickly. As a result, they miss the opportunity to wholeheartedly apologize or perhaps send the replacement phone right away via express delivery if you were counting on having the new phone in time for, say, an upcoming trip.

Customers in this situation may inadvertently contribute to the task orientation by telling the customer service rep, "I just want to get the phone I ordered." That may be a statement spoken out of frustration, yet it can also signal to the customer service rep that issuing the return authorization number is the most important task, since that is the first step in the company's normal procedure for getting the correct phone to the customer.

Sometimes, this task orientation can lead to reprehensible service. An estimated 14,000 people are mistakenly declared dead by the Social Security Administration each year. If you're one of them, it can be a financial nightmare, since your banking, credit cards, and credit reports are all tied to your Social Security number. As ridiculous as it may sound, the biggest hassle of all might be convincing a Social Security employee that you are still alive.

People victimized by this error report getting the runaround, having to make multiple trips to their local Social Security office, and being required to complete mountains of paperwork just to prove they aren't deceased.[1] Instead of receiving compassion, a heartfelt apology, and a swift resolution, the victims are frequently stonewalled by bureaucrats who view their primary role as complying with processing procedures. Fixing this error can take as long as two months, and it's even been reported that more paperwork is required to reinstate someone erroneously considered deceased than is needed to accidentally declare a person dead in the first place![2]

Sometimes, task orientation can lead to downright strange behavior. I once went into my local sporting goods store to get a pair of insoles for my running shoes. A sales associate approached me after I'd been browsing for a few minutes and asked if I needed assistance. I told him what I was looking for and asked if the insoles I had in my hand would fit the bill. He said they would and stuck a small sticker on the box.

"That was weird," I thought.

I browsed for a few more minutes and saw another brand of insoles that caught my eye. Suddenly, the sales associated reappeared. I showed him the box of insoles I'd just picked up and told him I was thinking of buying them instead of the first pair. Rather than commenting on whether

I was making a good decision, he said, "Okay, let me get a sticker on that." He put another small sticker on the new box.

I later learned that the store was trying to track how many sales were generated by each associate and the stickers corresponded to their ID numbers. The store manager had implemented the sticker program in an attempt to better monitor employee performance and, ultimately, learn how to boost sales, but the unintended result was emphasizing ID stickers over customer service. I can imagine the manager contributing to this task focus by issuing frequent reminders: "Don't forget to put your ID sticker on every product you sell so that you can get credit for the sale!"

The challenge, as we discussed in Chapter 7, is that tasks are usually easier to monitor than the outcomes. The manager at the sporting goods store would have had to spend more time on the sales floor observing sales associates to see which ones were truly helping customers and exhibiting good sales behaviors. The sticker program was enticing because it allowed the manager to use a sales report to track performance without ever leaving the office. The blind spot in this system, as was evident from my experience, was that affixing a sticker to an item a customer purchased wasn't necessarily an indicator that an associate had anything to do with generating that sale.

The cure for excessive task orientation is aligning employee responsibilities with the clearly defined customer service culture we discussed in Chapter 6. Employees should be focused on helping customers achieve their goals rather than following a set of rote procedures. Companies can take their service levels to new heights once their employees understand and embrace their role in delivering customer delight.

The Apple Store provides an excellent example of what can happen when employees focus intently on their customers. Unlike many other retailers where employees concentrate on pushing products, stocking shelves, or ringing up transactions, Apple Store employees are there to create a positive experience for their customers. They conduct product demonstrations, resolve technical problems, and help people get the most out of their MacBook, iPad, or other Apple product. According to Ron Johnson, the former Apple executive who created the Apple Store, every employee has one primary responsibility: "Their job is to figure out what you need and help you get it, even if it's a product Apple doesn't carry."[3]

The results of Apple's customer focus have been impressive. The Apple Store has become widely recognized for a high level of customer service, making *Bloomberg Businessweek*'s annual list of Customer Service Champs every year from 2007 to 2010.[4] This approach also translated into outstanding financial results, with retail analyst RetailSails reporting in 2011 that the Apple Store had the best sales per square foot of any U.S. retailer.[5] (Sales per square foot is a common measure of retail sales efficiency and is obtained by dividing a store's gross revenue by its square footage.)

Employees sometimes struggle to transition from being task-focused to becoming customer-focused, so I've developed a couple of exercises that can be used to change an employee's perspective. The first exercise requires members of a department or team to describe their role from their customer's point of view. In other words, what would you like your customers to say you do for them? Here are a few examples from some of my clients:

- Sales reps at a flower and plant wholesaler decided their role was helping florists (their primary customer) grow their businesses by helping them select flowers and plants that will sell well in their shops.

- Information technology employees working on a college campus determined that their role was helping faculty and staff minimize downtime from malfunctioning computers.

- Call center agents at a medical device manufacturer realized their role was helping to save lives by making sure the right products got to the right doctor in time to help the patients who need them.

The second exercise helps employees integrate this customer focus into their daily activities. Employees start by writing a thank-you letter from an imaginary customer addressing it to themselves. The letter should describe what the employee did and how it helped the customer. Here's an example from when I did the exercise myself:

Dear Jeff,

Thank you for being our trusted partner. Your commitment to helping us achieve our goals is the reason you are the first and only phone call when we need help improving customer service.

Thank you!

A. Client

Next, ask employees to read their thank-you letter at the start of each day for three weeks. They should think about what they would need to do for their customers to feel that way.

Finally, ask employees to try to get feedback from a customer that matches their letter. The feedback can be in the form of an actual letter, an e-mail, a response to a survey, or even a verbal compliment. When I did this exercise, I e-mailed a client and asked her if she would write a short testimonial for my website. I made no mention of my thank-you letter exercise, but her response was very close to what I had written in my fictitious letter. Here is what she wrote:

If I had to choose only one outside company to help with some training initiatives this year, that would be Toister Performance Solutions; Jeff is reliable, dependable, and flexible to incorporate the organizational culture in whatever he presents.

Extreme Role-Playing

In 1971, psychologist Philip G. Zimbardo conducted an experiment at Stanford University to observe the psychology of imprisonment. He recruited twenty-four male college students who were randomly divided into two groups. Members of one group were designated as prisoners while members of the other group were the prison guards. The study was intended to take place over the course of two weeks in a mock prison where the guards were instructed to watch over the prisoners.

What happened during the experiment took Zimbardo completely by surprise. Many of the students posing as prison guards soon began engaging in psychologically and even sexually abusive behavior toward the prisoners. Many of the prisoners began to exhibit signs of severe emotional distress. The results were so shocking that the experiment had to be halted after just six days.[6]

Zimbardo's controversial research revealed that ordinarily good people are capable of terrible things when they're put in the wrong environment. These situations start with an adversarial relationship between a group of evildoers and their victims that eventually worsens as people take small steps that unwittingly lead them to increasingly deplorable behavior. The behavior is allowed to continue because nobody in the group is either willing or able to recognize the path they are on and bring it to the attention of the other members.[7]

I certainly wouldn't put bad customer service on the same plane as the horrible acts that Zimbardo has studied, but his research can help us understand how ordinarily good employees can do terrible things to their customers.

Consider the example of the Transportation Security Administration (TSA). I'm a frequent traveler, and the majority of TSA agents I encounter are friendly and professional. They have a tough job, and most of them seem dedicated to helping provide a safe and efficient travel experience.

Unfortunately, there are a few TSA agents who subject passengers to rude and unfriendly treatment. The worst offenders have been accused of fondling, groping, and humiliating passengers through the use of security procedures put into effect in late 2010. In November of that year, the American Civil Liberties Union received more than 900 complaints from passengers who felt their civil rights had been violated by TSA agents. The complaints include descriptions of invasive pat-downs that were aggressively carried out in front of other travelers. Some of the complainants were so uncomfortable that they broke down in tears and vowed never to fly again.[8]

How can some TSA agents treat people so horribly? It starts with an "us" versus "them" approach, where some agents view their primary mission as compliance and crowd control. This effect is enhanced by the uniform and badge worn by TSA agents, which reinforces their position as authority figures.

Many of the TSA agents I come into contact with are polite, friendly, and helpful, but quite a few are taking those first few steps down the slippery slope of evil that Zimbardo describes. These individuals shout at passengers, issue seemingly arbitrary orders, and make demeaning statements about travelers they believe aren't complying quickly enough.

Zimbardo also noted that evil can flourish when it is passively accepted by members of the group. There have been several other TSA agents present each time I've encountered an abusive agent. The other agents were all within sight and earshot of the agent who was acting out of line, but none of them chose to intervene (at least not publicly). This sends a clear signal that the agent's inappropriate behavior is condoned, which increases the likelihood that the poor behavior will continue.

Another example of inhumane customer treatment is the infamous robo-signer home foreclosure scandal. The scandal erupted in the fall of 2010 when major lenders such as GMAC Mortgage were accused of employing people who indiscriminately signed off on thousands of foreclosure notices. These employees, dubbed "robo-signers," were approving documents that caused people to lose their homes while shirking their most important responsibility: verifying that no homes were mistakenly foreclosed upon.[9]

Jeffrey Stephan, one of the so-called robo-signers employed by GMAC, gave a deposition in one of the many ensuing lawsuits. His testimony illuminated a mix of factors that contributed to employees like him blindly signing off on thousands of foreclosures. He described how he would sign off on as many as 400 foreclosure notices per day, leaving little time to examine each one. There was no direct contact with homeowners, and Stephan looked solely at the figures presented in the foreclosure notices before signing them, so he was able to take a clinical approach without considering the consequences of his actions. He did his work by following procedures that he was taught through informal training and apparently never questioned what he was being asked to do. From his perspective, it was clear he thought his role was reviewing paperwork and not displacing families from their homes.[10]

TSA and GMAC are extreme examples, but smaller versions are encountered every day in customer service. There are plenty of employees who have come to believe their role is to stonewall, belittle, or otherwise treat their customers poorly. The lesson from Zimbardo's work is that these employees may not be the inherently bad people we believe them to be. Rather, they are part of an inherently bad system that brings out the worst in people.

Of course, it's also possible for an inherently good system to bring out the best in people. We've described in previous chapters how companies can make it easier for employees to focus on delighting their customers. Here are a few examples:

- Empower employees to be unreasonably generous to customers (Chapter 2).

- Put employees in a position where they are intrinsically motivated to do the right thing for their customers (Chapter 3).

- Eliminate policies that create conflict between customers and employees (Chapter 4).
- Root out systemic problems that cause poor service (Chapter 5).
- Create a customer-focused culture (Chapter 6).
- Make service a priority for all employees (Chapter 7).

This is a great start, but sometimes employees need a little more help understanding that service comes first. As an example, there's the case of the Transportation and Parking Department at Oregon Health and Science University (OHSU). Like many universities, parking at OHSU is in short supply, so it employs parking enforcement officers who are responsible for patrolling the various parking lots on campus and citing vehicles that are parked illegally.

However, the enforcement efforts were creating some customer service headaches. The citations issued generated numerous complaints and were frequently appealed. It got so bad that the department had to assign extra staff to handle the growing backlog of appeals. Even worse, the appeals process resulted in many of the citations being overturned, which meant that customers had been needlessly angered and inconvenienced.

Brett Dodson managed the enforcement team and wanted to improve customer service. He knew the key was for his team to spend more time engaging in dialogue with drivers, explaining rules, and providing friendly warnings rather than issuing so many citations. Many of his enforcement officers were having a hard time embracing this vision, though. They relished the opportunity to issue a violation and viewed their role as catching people parking where they shouldn't. A few of the enforcement officers would even watch for someone to park illegally and then wait until the driver left the vehicle so they could write a ticket rather than ask that person to park somewhere else.

Dodson decided to try a novel approach. For two months, enforcement officers weren't allowed to issue citations from 8:00 a.m. to 10:00 a.m. each day. These were the hours when most violations traditionally occurred, but Dodson sent his parking enforcement officers out without the handheld computers they needed to issue citations. Their handhelds were returned to them at 10:00 a.m., but they were told not to issue a citation unless they had first provided a warning.

It took a couple of months of ongoing effort, but eventually Dodson's work paid off. Individually, most parking enforcement officers learned to gain better compliance by educating drivers and offering alternatives. The number of appealed citations dropped significantly, freeing up the equivalent of two full-time employees to concentrate on other tasks. Even better, scores on the department's customer satisfaction survey improved dramatically.

Blind Obedience

Philip Zimbardo's research on what makes good people do evil things is hard for many people to accept. Most of us can't imagine sexually harassing a subject in a psychology experiment, yelling at confused travelers, or unthinkingly signing a document that will cause someone to lose her home. We'd like to believe we would take the high road and question authority when faced with one of those scenarios.

Another prominent psychologist, Stanley Milgram, demonstrated that under the right conditions the average person will blindly obey an order to do harm. Milgram conducted his classic obedience experiment in 1961. In it, subjects were instructed to give electric shocks to a person in an adjacent room whenever that person gave an incorrect answer to a memorization test. Unbeknownst to the subject, the person in the other room was actually an actor, and electric shocks weren't really being transmitted. The actor responded to the test questions using a push-button device that signaled the answer, but most of the questions were deliberately answered incorrectly.

The initial shocks were a mild 15 volts. The subjects were told to increase the voltage with each incorrect answer by turning a dial on an apparatus that had voltage designations ranging from 15 to 450. When the voltage reached 300, the subject heard the victim banging loudly on the wall of the adjacent room. The victim stopped responding entirely after the voltage reached 315 (labeled Extreme Intensity Shock on the dial), but the subjects were told to treat a nonresponse as an incorrect answer and continue administering the shocks. The shocks continued through 375 volts (Danger: Severe Shock) and even until the dial reached 450 volts (labeled XXX).

Incredibly, 65 percent of the subjects continued administering electric shocks all the way until the voltage reached the maximum 450. Nobody refused to participate in the electric shock experiment after being told about the initial setup, and every subject administered at least 300 volts. Only five out of forty subjects (12 percent) stopped their participation in the experiment when they heard the victim banging on the wall.

Most of the subjects became visibly uncomfortable, and many of them voiced concerns about what they were doing to the person administering the experiment. When subjects displayed signs of reluctance, the experimenter told subjects they must continue, and by and large they obeyed. These scary results show that people can easily be led to blindly follow directions, even when it should be obvious that those directions may result in harm.[11]

America Online (AOL) provides a real-world example of how blind obedience can result in ludicrous actions. In June 2006, Vincent Ferrari called AOL to cancel his membership. Over the course of a five-minute call, Ferrari repeatedly asked the AOL representative to cancel the membership. Instead of quickly handling the request, the customer service rep tried to talk Ferrari into remaining a member. When that didn't work, he resorted to talking down to Ferrari and stonewalling his request. Ferrari recorded the phone call and posted the audio to his blog, where it quickly went viral.[12]

This was not an isolated incident. Complaints about the treatment of customers trying to cancel AOL service had dogged the company for years. In 2004, two years before Ferrari posted the infamous customer service call on his blog, AOL settled several lawsuits from members who were still being billed after they tried to cancel their accounts.[13]

The poor treatment administered by AOL customer service representatives was a direct result of the way AOL handled account closures. In 2006, customers who wished to cancel their service were directed to a department called the "retention queue" and spoke with "retention consultants." These employees were paid bonuses to retain customers who called to cancel and were required to make a minimum of two retention offers before processing a cancellation request.[14] Clearly, the role of the retention consultant had nothing to do with outstanding customer service. It's hard to imagine another customer service scenario where employees are explicitly instructed to argue with a customer and encouraged to disregard reasonable requests.

What could happen if customer service representatives thought of disobeying a boss's order because they knew it would result in poor service? If you recall from Chapter 4, employees often weigh the risks and rewards of various options when their employer's poor policies cause them to choose between angering a customer or angering their boss. The risk/reward calculation might still make obedience the most likely option.

Larry (not his real name) worked as a customer service representative for a company in severe financial difficulty. The company was struggling to make payments to the contractors it relied on to serve clients. Larry and his coworkers received countless phone calls each day from angry contractors threatening to stop working until their past-due invoices were paid.

The payments weren't coming, but Larry was instructed to lie to contractors so they'd continue working. He was told to blame it on a paperwork error or on some other administrative delay. As a last resort, Larry could transfer the caller to a voice-mail box to leave a message for a manager—a manager Larry knew wouldn't be returning calls.

Treating contractors this way went against every customer service instinct Larry had, but he dutifully obeyed because disobeying orders could cost Larry his job. He had been unemployed for more than a year before he got this position, and he knew how tough the job market was. He considered himself lucky not to be among the employees who were recently laid off. Larry empathized with the unpaid contractors, but he had bills of his own to pay.

If you've read this far in the book, there's a good chance you are genuinely interested in delivering outstanding service. You can't envision yourself or your employees knowingly engaging in abusive acts toward your customers. The research conducted by Philip Zimbardo and Stanley Milgram suggests that otherwise-good people are capable of terrible acts when faced with a combination of the wrong conditions. So, the opposite must be true as well. You can steer your employees in the proper direction by creating the right conditions for outstanding service.

Many of these steps have already been covered in previous chapters or discussed elsewhere in this one, so there's no sense in rehashing everything. However, there are three reminders that I think are important for customer service leaders.

First, if you look closely at most customer service scandals, there is usually a company spokesperson who emphatically denies that poor customer treatment is the normal way of doing business. This action may seem noble on the surface, but what it really tells you is that either senior managers had no idea what was going on in their own company or they are distancing themselves from their employees in an effort to find a scapegoat. Chapter 4 discussed how important it is for leaders to have direct contact with customers and frontline employees. Having a genuine understanding of your customers' needs makes it far less likely that you'll ask your employees to carry out an unfair or unfavorable policy. You'll also be more attuned to your employees' behavior and can quickly guide them in the right direction if they get off course.

Second, leaders must be stewards of the company's customer service culture. As we discussed in Chapter 6, your policies, decisions, and approach to leading others will signal to employees whether you are truly committed to customer service. In the organizations we examined as examples, like the Social Security Administration, TSA, GMAC, or AOL, the customer was clearly unimportant to senior leaders at that time or else their widespread mistreatment of customers would never have happened. On the other hand, when service is a priority, such as at Apple or OHSU, organizations usually have results to prove they really do care about their customers.

Finally, leaders periodically find themselves having to prioritize between cost or customers. We'll cover this dilemma in greater detail in Chapter 11, but there have been plenty of examples throughout this book where a leader has chosen one over the other. GMAC wouldn't have allowed its employees to cut so many corners in order to foreclose on homes quickly and cheaply if these customers had been important to them, but it happened because company executives were committed to bolstering the bottom line. Conversely, OHSU wouldn't have forgone so much ticket revenue if it didn't believe it was more important to provide a high level of service to the thousands of faculty, staff, employees, patients, and guests who visited the campus every day.

Solution Summary: Helping Employees Establish the Right Roles

As the examples in this chapter illustrate, the service that employees provide is often dictated by the role they're playing. Great things can happen when employees understand their primary role is serving customers at the highest level. Getting employees to make that commitment requires a conscious decision and the right working conditions.

Here is a summary of the solutions that can help your customer service representatives make the right choice:

- Align employee responsibilities with your company's service philosophy so that they will naturally deliver outstanding service when they are doing their jobs correctly.

- Have employees write a description of their jobs and the value they provide to their customers.

- Use the "thank-you note" exercise to help employees integrate a customer focus into their daily activities.

- Take extreme measures, if necessary, to avoid poor customer treatment and to compel your customer service reps to find new ways to achieve results (recalling the example of OHSU taking away its parking enforcement officers' ability to write tickets so they would instead focus on educating the public to comply with parking rules). Avoid creating working conditions that could lead employees to subject their customers to poor treatment by maintaining a direct connection to customers and frontline employees, acting as a steward of your organization's customer-focused culture, and understanding when to prioritize service over short-term cost efficiency.

Notes

1. Blake Ellis, "Social Security Wrongly Declares 14,000 People Dead Each Year," *CNNMoney.com*, August 22, 2011.

2. Alex Johnson and Nancy Amons, " 'Resurrected,' but Still Wallowing in Red Tape," *MSNBC.com*, February 29, 2008.

3. Ron Johnson, "What I Learned Building the Apple Store," HBR Blog Network, *Harvard Business Review*, November 21, 2011.

4. According to *Bloomberg Businessweek*'s annual list of Customer Service Champs at www.businessweek.com, Apple was ranked No. 18 in 2007, No. 21 in 2008, No. 20 in 2009, and No. 3 in 2010. The *Bloomberg Businessweek* list was compiled each year from 2007 to 2010 in conjunction with data from J.D. Power and Associates and its own reader surveys.

5. "RetailSails Exclusive: Ranking U.S. Chains by Retail Sales per Square Foot," news release, August 23, 2011; http://retailsails.com/2011/08/23/retailsails-exclusive-ranking-u-s-chains-by-retail-sales-per-square-foot/.

6. There is a wealth of information about this study on the Stanford Prison Experiment website: www.prisonexp.org.

7. Philip Zimbardo's presentation at the 2008 TED (Technology, Entertainment, Design) Conference provides a good overview of his extensive research; see "Philip Zimbardo Shows How People Become Monsters . . . or Heroes," http://www.ted.com/index.php/talks/philip_zimbardo_on_the_psychology_of_evil.html.

8. American Civil Liberties Union, "ACLU Reports More Than 900 Complaints This Month over Enhanced TSA Security Measures," news release, November 24, 2010.

9. David Streitfeld, "Bank of America to Freeze Foreclosure Cases," *New York Times,* October 1, 2010.

10. Oral deposition of Jeffrey D. Stephan, Maine District Court, District 9, Federal National Mortgage Association v. Bradbury and GMAC Mortgage, LLC, June 7, 2010.

11. Stanley Milgram, "Behavioral Study of Obedience," *Journal of Abnormal and Social Psychology* 67 (1963), pp. 371–378.

12. Randall Stross, "AOL Said, 'If You Leave Me I'll Do Something Crazy,'" *New York Times,* July 2, 2006.

13. Juan Carlos Perez, "AOL Settles Billing Lawsuits," *PCWorld.com,* June 4, 2004.

14. Stross, "AOL Said, 'If You Leave Me I'll Do Something Crazy'."

CHAPTER 9

The Problem with Empathy

Encouraging Employees to Empathize
with Their Customers

The Cheese Plate Incident is a customer service story that will forever be infamous in my family. It's hard to imagine a plate of cheese causing so much trouble, but the real problem was a lack of empathy that made a simple error comically worse.

My wife and I, along with my parents and in-laws, were staying at a hotel in Phoenix while we were in town to attend a few spring training baseball games. One night, the six of us decided to order a meat and cheese plate from room service to have as an appetizer as we all enjoyed a glass of wine before going out to dinner. My wife called to place the order and verified the contents of the meat and cheese plate since a few of us have food allergies. The room service associate told my wife that the meat selection was currently unavailable but offered to send up a plate of assorted cheeses and crackers instead. My wife agreed to the substitution after making sure it wouldn't trigger anyone's allergies.

A room service attendant arrived with the cheese plate approximately thirty minutes later. Unfortunately, she left the room before we noticed that the platter also contained salmon, which was a problem because a family member is allergic to seafood. This was puzzling because my wife had specifically mentioned food allergies when she placed the order, and had carefully verified the ingredients to ensure the appetizer would be safe for everyone to enjoy.

I called room service to request a replacement. The hotel associate thought she'd done us a favor by adding the salmon and didn't seem to understand that the salmon could have made someone very ill. She wasn't particularly apologetic but did agree to send up a cheese plate like the one we'd originally ordered.

We waited another thirty minutes, but the second cheese plate didn't arrive. By now it had been an hour since we'd placed our original order so we were getting hungry and impatient. I called room service again and was told our order was delayed because the kitchen was backed up with other orders. The associate promised to send the cheese tray up right away, but it was annoying to have to wait so long since our original order had been incorrect.

Another fifteen minutes passed, and still no cheese plate. It would soon be time for us to leave for dinner, so my wife called to see if the cheese plate was on its way. It still hadn't left the kitchen, so she canceled the order. Once again the hotel associate wasn't particularly apologetic, but she did agree not to charge us for the appetizer since they had never delivered the correct order.

The next evening, when we returned to our hotel room after a day at the ballpark, we were surprised to find a plate of cheese and crackers in our room with a note apologizing for the mistake from the night before. Unfortunately, it looked like the plate had been sitting out for quite some time since the cheese was in bad shape. Even if the cheese plate had been fresh, it would have gone to waste since we were heading straight out to dinner. At that point all we could do was laugh at how absurd the Cheese Plate Incident had become.

Throughout the experience, our frustration and disappointment arose from a lack of empathy. Adding the salmon to the original order demonstrated that the hotel associate didn't understand our concern about food allergies. Failing to apologize or expedite the replacement showed us she didn't care that we might be irritated by the error—or that we might be hungry! Admitting that the replacement was delayed by other orders told us we weren't a priority. I imagine she thought she'd recovered by sending us a cheese plate and an apology card the following evening, but in reality, it felt like salt on the wound because it went to waste.

In this chapter, we'll see that service failures like the one I've just described often happen because empathy is a difficult skill for employees to master. Many employees lack the fundamental experiences upon which empathy is built. They find it hard to understand their customers' emotions, or they may fail to grasp the importance of addressing these emotions when a service failure occurs. They may not even realize that their customers' perspective is different from their own and miss out on opportunities to serve because they can only see the world through their own eyes. The good news is that customer service representatives can learn to be more empathetic, but it involves careful training and a patient supervisor.

The Source of Empathy

Empathy is a customer service skill that allows people to avoid frustrating situations by seeing things from their customers' perspective. It allows them to understand how the customer is thinking and feeling in a given situation, and take steps to ensure the customer is satisfied. Without empathy, employees may see problems differently than their customers or perhaps not see the problems at all.

The ability to empathize with another person comes from having had a similar or closely related experience. You're able to understand what the other person is thinking and feeling because you've been there yourself, or you've experienced something that was close enough. For example, if you've ever accidentally touched a hot iron you're likely to wince if you see someone accidently touch a hot stove.[1]

Many employees struggle to empathize with customers because they don't have a similar experience they can relate to. An accountant probably does her own taxes, so she may not understand the confusion her clients experience when they try to fill out tax forms. A person answering a tech support hotline likely fixes his own computer, so he might have trouble understanding the helplessness his customers feel when their computers stop working. There's a good chance that a valet parking a $100,000 sports car doesn't understand the anxiety a customer feels when entrusting something so expensive to a stranger.

A lack of related experience might have been one of the causes of the Cheese Plate Incident. The guest service associate might not have realized that seafood is a common allergen if she didn't have food allergies herself. She might not have understood that the replacement cheese plate needed to be expedited if she didn't have the experience to know hotel guests ordering appetizers are likely to have other plans that evening. When she had a replacement cheese plate delivered the next day, it probably wouldn't occur to her that we might not be there to enjoy it if she didn't travel often enough to understand that guests don't always keep the same schedule.

Perhaps what's most confounding about empathy is how obvious the problem seems to those of us who *can* relate to the situation. Employees who have had similar experiences are often naturally able to empathize with their customers in a way that other employees can't. I frequently see young mothers traveling on airplanes with fussy infants, and the most helpful flight attendants are consistently those who are mothers themselves. They understand the difficulties of traveling with an infant and are able tell the young mother, "Here's what I did when my kids were that age."

The easiest customers to serve are frequently people who have worked in similar positions and can empathize with the employee who is assisting them. Friends of mine who spent years working as food servers always make a point to tip generously because they know tips are an important part of a server's income. People who have worked in call centers often try to be extra polite and patient with the person on the other end of the line because they understand how stressful the job can be. When I try on clothes in a store, I always clear out my dressing room because clearing out dressing rooms was the chore I enjoyed least when I worked in retail.

If empathy comes from having had similar experiences, the easiest way to help customer service employees become more empathetic is to put them in their customers' shoes.

One way is through training. Many upscale hotels have associates spend a night as a guest so that they can see things from their guests' point of view. The Westin Portland has new hires participate in what's called an Associate Stay Experience within their first ninety days on the job. They're given a checklist of experiences to observe, including the reservation process, their arrival at the hotel, and ordering a meal from in-room dining. Afterward, associates debrief with their supervisors and give feedback about their stay. This training allows associates to have a genuine understanding of what it's like to be a guest at the hotel.

Another way to put employees in their customers' shoes is through sharing personal stories from customers. Stories are a powerful way of tapping into our imaginations and helping us understand how the characters may have felt or what they were thinking. I've worked with several clients who make medical devices, and they all use a similar technique to help employees empathize with their customers. Throughout their offices you'll find posters picturing real patients who have been helped by their products. The posters offer a brief description of a patient's disease or injury and explain how a particular product helped improve or even saved the person's life.

These examples remind employees of the importance of what they're doing. And even if they don't have direct patient contact, they go to work each day knowing they are positively impacting other people's lives. In many cases, the stories also remind employees of a friend or family member who may have faced a similar medical ordeal.

A third option is to hire employees who already have similar experiences to those of the customers they'll be serving. One of the reasons I enjoy shopping at the sporting goods retailer REI is that the employees who work there tend to be avid users of the equipment they sell. When my wife and I went there to buy backpacks for a hiking trip, the associate who helped us was an experienced backpacker who understood the nervousness of planning a first-time wilderness expedition. He helped us select the right gear, and more important, he took extra time to reassure us about our plans.

Communicating on Different Levels

Empathy can also be a challenge because customers and customer service representatives often rely on different parts of their brain as they communicate with each other.

Customers tend to engage the part of their brain that regulates emotions, especially when they feel that something is going wrong. A 2011 study by Bård Tronvoll published in the *Journal of Service Management* found that 97 percent of customers have negative emotions such as frustration, anger, or helplessness when they experience a service failure.[2] From the customer's perspective, empathizing with negative emotions is an important part of the solution when a service failure is being addressed.

Unfortunately, negative emotions often go undetected or unacknowledged by employees who are focused on finding a rational solution to their customer's problem. Without empathy, employees will have a difficult time understanding how the customer is feeling because rational thinking and emotions are controlled by two separate parts of our brain. When customer service reps are unable to experience the customer's emotions, it's easier for them to engage the part of their brain that regulates rational thinking as they try to deliver service.[3]

When I received an e-mail with a discount offer from an online shoe retailer and it happened to be time for me to buy some new running shoes, I clicked on the e-mail link, went to the website, and picked out a pair. However, my promised discount wasn't deducted from my order total. I still wanted the shoes, so I sent an e-mail to the customer service department to see if someone could complete my order and apply the discount.

The next day I received a response from Adam in the customer service department. He told me that to receive the discount, I would have to call the company's toll-free hotline and place my order over the phone with a customer service representative. He reminded me to explain the situation and told me the rep would honor the promotion.

Adam was clearly communicating with me on a rational level. From that perspective, my problem was solved. I needed to know how to take advantage of the promotion when placing my order, and he had provided that information.

But Adam's response did little to make me feel better about the experience. I was frustrated by the initial problem. Now I was annoyed by the additional hassle of having to call the customer service department. I was also irritated that Adam had passed my problem off to someone else.

Fortunately, the opposite experience occurred when I called the customer service line to place my order. The customer service rep, Laura, was friendly and apologetic, and her empathetic response to my situation instantly made me feel better. While placing the order, I told Laura that I was going to be out of town in a few days and was concerned that my shoes would be delivered while I was away. She assured me that she understood and would make sure the delivery was timed to arrive on a day when I would be home to receive it. To my surprise, my shoes arrived just two days later. Laura had upgraded my shipping to express delivery at no extra charge. Her empathetic approach turned a negative experience into a very positive one.

Why did Laura succeed where Adam failed? While Adam simply provided information, Laura addressed how I felt. She acknowledged and apologized for my frustration. She instilled confidence that she would be able to handle the situation with minimal hassle. Best of all, she understood my concerns about having a package sitting on my doorstep while I was out of town and took steps to ensure that didn't happen.

Service failures occur every day when employees offer rational solutions without addressing their customers' underlying emotions. The restaurant manager who offers a free dessert when a customer complains about too much dressing on a salad may embarrass someone who is watching his weight. She'd likely get better results by offering a sincere apology to the customer and expediting a replacement salad with the dressing on the side so the customer could add dressing to his liking. An appliance repair technician may think he did a great job when he got his customer's washing machine running again, but may not notice the customer is irritated that the technician arrived forty-five minutes late. The repair technician could make a better recovery by empathizing with the inconvenience the customer suffered from a late service call, on top of having a broken appliance, and apologize profusely. A doctor who prescribes a routine blood test may add to a patient's anxiety if she doesn't sense the patient's nervousness about what the test results may reveal. The doctor would make the patient feel much better if she took a few moments to explain the purpose of the tests and offer a realistic view of what the results may indicate.

According to psychologist Guy Winch, we often experience a need to have our emotions validated when we get angry or upset. We want the other person to understand why we feel the way we do and to acknowledge that our feelings are reasonable, given the situation. Having our emotions validated can bring instant relief and make us feel better.[4]

Customers who experience a problem may get even more upset when their emotions aren't validated or their feelings are ignored, such as when a customer service rep focuses on providing a rational solution to a problem without sincerely apologizing. These situations highlight how customers and employees often communicate on different levels, with the customer getting angrier because of an employee's seeming lack of empathy and the employee getting confused by the customer who seems to get more irate the more the employee tries to provide a solution.

Chapter 2 discussed ways that unreasonable customers can be an obstacle to outstanding service. One of the reasons customers become unreasonable is the emotional part of our brain has the ability to hijack rational thinking. Exceptionally strong emotions such as frustration, anger, or even shame can cloud our ability to reason and impair our judgment.

This means that taking a rational approach to an extremely upset customer can be like pouring gas on a fire. I once watched a hotel guest fly off the handle when he tried to check into the hotel and was told that he had no reservation and that the hotel was sold out for the evening. He insisted he had a confirmed reservation and demanded that the hotel find him a room. The guest started yelling at the front desk associate and slamming his hand on the counter as his frustration steadily increased.

The front desk associate made the mistake of focusing on rational solutions rather than first diffusing the guest's extreme anger. She suggested that an error might have been made when the guest made his reservation, but this tactic just made him more furious. The guest yelled even louder when the associate offered to accommodate him at a nearby hotel. A manager finally stepped in to address the situation but made things worse by telling the man, "Sir, I'm going to have to ask you to calm down." This comment made the guest so irate that the hotel's security officer had to intervene.

The front desk associate at the hotel may have diffused the situation by taking a moment to empathize with a tired and frustrated traveler. Rather than trying to prove the guest was wrong and she was right, she might have started the discussion by apologizing for the situation and indicated that he was perfectly right to feel frustrated. She shouldn't have continued to offer solutions until she could help the guest overcome his initial surprise and anger. If he was still extremely agitated, the associate could then call her manager over so the manager could speak with the guest privately to find a solution.

Customer service employees can learn to identify and address their customers' emotional needs in situations like this one, but it should never be left to chance. It takes training and practice to help employees empathize with their customers. There are also some things you simply have to experience firsthand to learn, such as the fact that telling an irate customer to calm down will almost certainly have the opposite effect!

Here's a simple exercise you can use to help employees develop their empathic skills. Start by picking a situation where your customers are likely to get angry, upset, or confused. For example, employees in a furniture store may find that customers are disappointed or frustrated if a piece of furniture they ordered doesn't arrive by the expected delivery date.

Next, have employees think of a situation when they encountered a similar problem and ask them to describe how they felt when it happened. The furniture store employees might recall a time when they ordered something that didn't arrive on time, which could be anything from a piece of furniture to a pizza. The typical emotions they experienced as a result might range from disappointment to frustration and even anger if the delay caused additional inconvenience.

Finally, help employees brainstorm ways they can help customers avoid experiencing similar emotions. In the case of the furniture store employees, this exercise might help them realize that a sincere and heartfelt apology is necessary when an order is delayed. To make up for the inconvenience caused by the delay, they may need to bend the rules by offering a more precise delivery time than the four-hour window called for by company policy. Or perhaps they can discount or waive the delivery fee to make it up to the customer.

Another technique that employees can use to neutralize negative emotions is called the "preemptive acknowledgment." This technique involves identifying a situation that may provoke a customer's negative emotions *before* the customer gets upset. The preemptive acknowledgment allows an employee to acknowledge a service failure and suggest a solution without the customer ever becoming angry.

Here's a scenario we've all experienced that highlights how powerful the preemptive acknowledgment can be. Imagine you are dining at a busy restaurant. You and your party place your orders and engage in lively conversation while waiting for your dinner. After a while, your growling stomach reminds you that it's taking a long time for your meal to arrive. You notice your water glass is empty, and then realize the people at the table next to you are enjoying their food, even though they were seated ten minutes after you were. To make matters worse, you have to flag down another server to get an update since yours is suddenly nowhere to be found. Everyone at the table is irritated by the time the food finally arrives.

Now, let's look at the same situation with the only difference being that your server uses the preemptive acknowledgment. You're dining at a busy restaurant and enjoying lively conversation after placing your order. After a while, your growling stomach reminds you that it's taking a long time for your food to arrive. Just then, your server arrives at your table and politely interrupts your conversation.

"I'm so sorry for the delay," the server says. "I just checked with the kitchen, and your order is the next one up. In the meantime, may I refill your drinks?"

Everyone at the table thanks your server for checking in and refilling their drinks. The server returns a few minutes later with everyone's food. The short delay is completely forgotten as you enjoy your meal.

The preemptive acknowledgment is effective because it prevents customers' negative emotions from hijacking their rational thinking. A meal that takes ten minutes too long to arrive hardly qualifies as the worst customer service ever, but an emotional cocktail of hunger, irritation, and a sense of unfair treatment can make it seem that way. Avoiding these strong emotions allows customers to keep their good humor and maintain an appropriate perspective.

Training employees to use the preemptive acknowledgment has the extra benefit of helping employees become more observant of their customers' needs. By paying close attention and learning to be more observant, the restaurant server would realize when a table of customers has been waiting too long for their meal. This realization prompts the server to check on the order in the kitchen, which in turn allows her to apologize to the guests for the delay and provide an update.

Self-Centered Behavior That Leads to Poor Service

Expressing empathy requires us to view things from the other person's perspective, but this can be challenging because our natural perspective is our own.

Notice what happens the next time a cashier hands you your change. Does he put the bills in your palm with the coins on top, making it hard for you to grab the loose coins? Or does he put the coins in your palm first, and then place the bills on top?

Most cashiers will collect the coins from their register first and then grab the necessary bills while the coins sit in the palm of their hand. It's easier to do it this way because coins are harder to pick up when you have a handful of bills. If the cashier simply turns his hand over to place the change in the customer's hand, the bills will be in the customer's palm and the coins will sit on top of the bills. It's a very efficient maneuver, but it also makes the coins harder for the customer to corral.

Some cashiers realize that if it's difficult for them to hold coins on top of the bills in their hand, it will be difficult for their customers, too. They place the coins in their customer's palm first and then the bills on top. It takes the slightest bit of extra effort, but the result is that customers spend less time fumbling with their change or dropping coins.

Using empathy to see things from a customer's perspective can be difficult under normal circumstances, but it becomes extremely tough for customer service employees when their own emotions are running high.

My wife and I experienced this situation while vacationing in San Francisco when we visited a bar that had been recommended by several friends. The bar was packed when we arrived, and we were fortunate to snag the last open table. When our server finally made it over to take our drink order, we could tell by the look on her face that she was overwhelmed by the crowd.

Our server returned about twenty minutes later and brusquely dropped two drinks on our table. Unfortunately, they weren't our drinks. "Excuse me," I said. "I don't think this is what we ordered."

The server looked at the drinks and then exclaimed, "Aw shit!"

We sat in stunned silence as she scooped up the drinks without saying another word. It took another twenty minutes for her to return with our correct order. She put the drinks on our table and quickly left without apologizing for the error, the delay, or her exclamation.

This server's customer service was inexcusable, but we could do our own empathy exercise to better understand her behavior. Think of a time when you felt overwhelmed by work and were so busy you barely had time to think. You probably developed a sort of tunnel vision where you blocked out all other distractions so that you could focus on the unending tasks at hand. I know whenever I try this trick, I'm able to accomplish more work, yet I also become more abrupt with the people around me.

Now think about our bar server: If she was experiencing this type of stress-induced tunnel vision, it was probably a major setback for her to find out she delivered an incorrect drink order to our table. Her natural inclination would be to feel even more stress, and perhaps a little helpless, when she discovered she'd need to make an extra trip to the bar to correct our order. Our mild disappointment at being served the wrong drinks had no chance of showing up on her radar.

This type of scenario is often at the core of really bad customer service. The customer feels some type of negative emotion because of a service failure, but the employee doesn't acknowledge the customer's feelings because she's experiencing her own negative emotions. This causes customers to get even more upset because they're confronted with a bad employee attitude rather than the validation they needed.

Chapter 5 revealed ways that poor products, processes, and procedures can contribute to employee dissatisfaction. A company that has these types of chronic service failures will find it difficult to have empathetic customer service representatives. Over time, the employees' own feelings of frustration and helplessness, arising from repeatedly handling the same problems, will cause them to stop observing or caring about their customers' feelings.

Companies that are going out of business provide a prime example of what can happen when employees' emotions make it challenging for them to serve their customers. When the book retailer Borders announced in July 2011 that it was closing its stores and liquidating the company, a change happened among many of its employees. Suddenly faced with the prospect of losing their jobs, associates decided to let their customers know how they really felt. There was a much-publicized incident involving employees at the Borders in Mansfield, Massachusetts, who posted a handwritten sign to customers that read: "Things we never told you: Ode to a bookstore death." The sign listed sixteen grievances about their customers, including questions they thought were stupid, gripes about their customers' taste in literature, and complaints about customers' shopping habits.[5]

In any situation, overcoming the obstacle of empathy requires a solution that adopts the customer's perspective at the employee, managerial, and organizational levels.

At the employee level, training must be provided to help people understand the customer's point of view. For instance, cashiers should be trained to give change by first putting the coins in their customer's hand and then placing the bills on top. This was the first lesson I learned when I was trained to be a cashier, and no doubt it would have taken me a long time to learn it on my own if my trainer hadn't emphasized its importance.

At the managerial level, customer service supervisors must empathize with their employees as well as with their customers. They must understand that the job of providing service can sometimes cause frustration, irritation, and other negative emotions. Leaders who fail to recognize their employees' emotions run the risk of having those emotions hijack their employees' ability to empathize with customers.

When I was a customer service manager, I learned it was important to let my reps vent for a few minutes after working with a particularly difficult customer. This let them get it off their chest without taking it out on the next person they served. It also let my employees know that I acknowledged their feelings. The catch was that I insisted that we end the conversation by discussing strategies for dealing with similar customers in the future, so my employees could learn from their experiences.

At the organizational level, companies need to work to eliminate sources of employee angst that might make it difficult for them to empathize with customers. Specifically, companies must eliminate those products, processes, and procedures, as discussed in Chapter 5, that systematically result in poor service. For example, if the bar that my wife and I visited in San Francisco was chronically understaffed, the managers would need to hire and train more capable servers to work each shift or else risk burning out their employees and turning away customers who experienced slow and surly service.

Solution Summary: Helping Employees Demonstrate Empathy with Customers

Empathy doesn't always come naturally to employees, but they can learn to understand and validate their customers' emotions. Here is a short summary of the solutions presented in this chapter:

- Help your employees develop relevant, related experiences they can use to empathize with customers, such as giving them the opportunity to be customers themselves.

- Share stories and testimonials from real customers to remind your employees how delivering great service can make their customers feel understood and acknowledged.

- Hire employees who use your product or service, so they can easily relate to the people they serve.

- Train employees to understand how customers feel when they encounter a problem by asking employees to recall a similar experience they've had. Have them describe how the experience made them feel, then discuss ways they can help their customers avoid those negative feelings.

- Teach employees to use the preemptive acknowledgment as a technique to diffuse the negative emotions of customers before they explode.

- Show employees how to deliver service from their customers' perspective; you can start by demonstrating the correct way to hand change to a customer.

- Demonstrate empathy toward your employees when they experience negative emotions, to validate their feelings and prevent them from taking out their frustrations on a customer.

- Eliminate the sources of employee angst that could cause them to fail to identify and react to their customers' negative emotions.

Notes

1. Jean Decety and Philip L. Jackson. "A Social-Neuroscience Perspective on Empathy," *Current Directions in Psychological Science* 15, no 2 (2006), pp. 54–58.

2. B. Tronvoll, "Negative Emotions and Their Effect on Customer Complaint Behaviour," *Journal of Service Management*, 22, no. 1 (2011), pp. 111–134.

3. Daniel Goleman, *Working with Emotional Intelligence* (New York: Bantam Books, 1998).

4. Guy Winch, "The Antidote to Anger and Frustration," The Squeaky Wheel (blog), *Psychology Today,* June 18, 2011.

5. Patrick Anderson, "Borders Gets the Last Word," *The (Attleboro, MA) Sun Chronicle,* September 22, 2011.

CHAPTER 10

Emotional Roadblocks

Helping Employees Overcome Their Own Emotions

One of my lowest moments in customer service was when I deliberately hung up on a customer, knowing full well that if she called back and asked to speak to the manager she would get me on the phone once again.

It wasn't the right way to handle things and I learned from the experience, but in that particular moment I let my emotions get the best of me. It wasn't really that specific customer who set me off. A swirl of negative emotions had been building for quite some time, and this person was just the spark that ignited the blaze.

For starters, I didn't like my job. I had accepted the position as the customer service manager for a small catalog company six months earlier, because my wife and I were moving to San Diego from Boston. I moved out first to get a job so that we'd have at least one income as we settled into our new hometown. It was the best job I could get in the three weeks budgeted for my job search, but I wouldn't otherwise have chosen to work for this company. Even during the interview process I had the sense it was going to be a difficult place to work.

If you've ever had a bad boss, you know how hard it can be to go to work each day. I had two bad bosses: the company's owners—who were also the president and CFO. They didn't communicate well and often gave conflicting orders that pulled me in different directions, so I was constantly confused about my job responsibilities and main priorities. The company president was particularly unfriendly and angered easily.

The day I hung up on the customer was a week before Christmas. A perfect storm of three problems converged to cause a deluge of angry calls that went far beyond what you'd expect during the normal holiday rush. First, many of our most popular items were backordered and our supplier had just informed us that a delivery that could allow us to fill many orders would not arrive before Christmas, as we had expected. Second, major blizzards throughout the country had caused many shipments to be delayed or lost. Third, poor process control in our warehouse contributed to an extraordinarily high number of shipping errors, where packages were sent with the wrong item or to the wrong address. My whole team was working long hours and facing an enormous amount of stress.

On this particular day I'd already spent eight hours on the phone because we were drowning in calls. An alarm would sound throughout the entire company whenever a customer was on hold for more than a minute, and everyone in the company was expected to answer the phones when the alarm went off. My coworkers in other departments were frustrated with me because they were spending much of their day on the phone instead of doing their normal work. The president wouldn't allow me to change the alarm setting to keep customers on hold longer before it sounded off, but even he was sending me angry e-mails because he too was spending a chunk of his day on the phone. However, I was completely powerless to stop the flood of callers.

I finally hit my boiling point with one particular customer. She was yelling insults at me as I tried in vain to apologize and find a solution. *Click.* I hung up.

I'm not proud of my action in that moment, but I'm grateful for the experience because it helped me fully understand how difficult customer service can be. Everyone who's spent more than a few days in customer service has had similar experiences. After all, we're all human!

In this chapter, we'll look at ways that employees' emotions can negatively affect their performance. We'll see how our instinctive reaction when someone is yelling at us can easily lead to poor service. We'll discover that negative emotions are contagious and can spread from customers to employees. Finally, we'll examine how difficult it can be to smile when we just don't feel like smiling. Companies that are committed to outstanding service must make it easy for their employees to be happy and help employees to develop skills to work through situations when they experience the negative emotions that come with the job.

"Don't Take It Personally" Is Bad Advice

I can't count how many times I've heard someone say, "Don't take it personally" to an employee who's upset after working with a difficult customer. I'm sure I've said it myself a few times. You may have had the same thought about me as you read my story at the beginning of this chapter.

But our natural instinct is to take things personally when other people are directing their anger or frustration at us. We're likely to experience emotions such as anger, embarrassment, or even fear that can cause us to lash out at the other person or find a way to retreat. Expecting people to dismiss this normal reaction is like telling them not to laugh when they hear a funny joke or not to be concerned when they learn a family member has lost his job. It takes effort and training for employees to learn to manage their emotional reactions.

To understand why this happens, it's helpful to turn to the work of Abraham Maslow, a psychologist famous for developing a list of factors that motivate people, often referred to as Maslow's hierarchy of human needs. This framework describes our basic motivators in order of priority, where the first priority must be satisfied before we can be motivated by the next priority. For example, humans have a strong desire to be safe from physical harm, but people who have unmet physiological needs for food, water, or sleep would be willing to put their safety at risk in an effort to survive.[1] Here is Maslow's list of needs, in priority order:

1. Physiological

2. Safety

3. Love and belonging

4. Esteem

5. Self-actualization

I've trained thousands of customer service employees, and nearly all of them have a strong desire to be good at what they do. This intent fits squarely with self-actualization, which means the ability to perform at the peak of one's abilities. However, people are motivated to be the best they can be only when all their higher-priority needs are being met. A customer directing a verbal tirade at an employee challenges the employee's self-esteem, so the employee's motivation to help the upset customer becomes a lower priority related to the need to protect his own self-esteem.

For example, here's a real story from Paul, who was working in the office at a nightclub when he received a phone call from a customer who was upset because his credit card company had detected a fraudulent charge. The customer was convinced that a server at the club had stolen his credit card number. At first Paul tried his best to be helpful, but he quickly realized the man just wanted to vent. The customer's repeated accusations, "Your server stole my credit card number" and "You guys need to be more careful," soon wore thin. As Paul explained, "I could feel my blood pressure going up. I could feel my face get flush. I felt like, 'Don't accuse my coworker of doing something that you don't know that they did.' There are a million ways that credit card numbers get stolen. It was so frustrating to me."

The customer's uncooperative approach made it difficult for Paul to manage his emotions, despite his years of experience in the hospitality industry. It was insulting to hear the customer accuse one of his coworkers of a crime without providing a shred of evidence. The caller also repeatedly used the word *you*, which could have meant "the club," but it was tough for Paul to avoid feeling like it was a personal attack.

Toward the end of the call, Paul stopped worrying about helping the customer because, he said, "I got to the point where I was so done with him. I started doing everything I could to get him off the phone."

Working with upset customers is difficult, but it is even more challenging for employees to manage their emotions when they have a boss or coworkers who are unsupportive. The social structure provided by the workplace is a powerful part of most employees' lives, and it's often been noted that we spend more time with our coworkers than we do with our own families. This makes it vitally important that we have a sense of belonging at work, since—according to Maslow's hierarchy—the human desire for love and acceptance is a more powerful motivator than esteem or self-actualization.

The day I hung up on my customer, I was having a hard time managing my emotions because two important needs weren't being met. The customer's tirade challenged my sense of self-esteem and frustrated me because I felt she was more interested in insulting me than in letting me try to assist her. Even worse, I was affected by a toxic work environment at a job I couldn't stand, a boss who was angry at me for reasons I felt were his own doing, and coworkers who were frustrated with me, too. I experienced no sense of belonging during that moment and stopped caring about whether I did a good job.

A 2011 study by researchers at Bowling Green State University found a correlation between employee performance and the extent to which employees are subjected to mistreatment from customers and coworkers. The study, which focused on bank tellers at a regional bank, found that tellers who reported high levels of customer and coworker incivility were absent from work at least one more day per month than their colleagues. These same employees also experienced a 13 percent decrease in sales performance (as measured by their opening new accounts and selling additional products to customers).[2]

Clearly, companies need to offer their employees more than pithy advice to help them avoid resorting to poor service when confronted by an angry or upset customer. Employees need a supportive work environment that encourages their commitment to the team. They must also be helped to develop the skills they need to handle upset customers more effectively.

Companies that consistently deliver outstanding service base their success on a counterintuitive approach: They emphasize that employees, not customers, are most important. In Chapter 2, we discussed the importance of protecting employees from abusive customers as a way to encourage loyalty and commitment. Putting employees first promotes a sense of belonging and high self-esteem that ultimately leads to more positive relationships with both customers and coworkers.

Starbucks is an example of a company that embraces an employee-first philosophy. The company's CEO, Howard Schultz, describes Starbucks employees as being central to the customer's experience. "That experience can come to life only if people are proud, if they respect and trust the green apron and the people they are representing," he has said publicly.[3] This approach helps to explain why Starbucks appears regularly on both *Fortune Magazine*'s annual list of the 100 Best Companies to Work For[4] and *Bloomberg Businessweek*'s annual Customer Service Champs list.[5]

I happen to be sitting in my local Starbucks as I write this passage. There are happy customers at every table and a line of people waiting to get their coffee. The employees cheerfully greet each customer and know many of the regulars' orders by heart. The baristas expertly produce each person's drink, dispense coffee, serve food, and ring up transactions in what looks like a well-choreographed dance behind the counter. This environment is created by coworkers who clearly like each other, their jobs, and the company they work for.

Of course, all customer service employees will occasionally encounter a customer whose anger is hard to handle. Effective customer service leaders keep in mind how difficult it is for employees to manage their emotions in these situations. Employees who are giving their best effort will benefit from a supervisor who helps them approach a customer service incident as a learning experience rather than a reason to take disciplinary action. A leader who is too quick to punish employees who give honest effort will likely lose their respect, so punitive measures such as written warnings, suspensions, and terminations are best reserved for willful acts of egregiously poor service, disastrous lapses in judgment, or an inability to learn from repeated mistakes.

There are three things that supervisors can do to help their employees learn from experience and improve their ability to manage their emotions in stressful situations. First, the supervisor should help the employee evaluate the situation and determine why the customer was angry. The intent isn't to place blame, but rather to diagnose the root cause.

Second, the supervisor and employee should discuss strategies for getting better results when the employee encounters a similar situation in the future. Could the employee do or say something a little differently? Is there an opportunity to diffuse the customer's anger before it boils over?

Finally, the supervisor should encourage employees to apply these new strategies on the job. This supportive approach will make employees more likely to be forthcoming, asking their supervisor for help rather than trying to prevent the boss from hearing about an incident with a difficult customer. It also fosters a spirit of continuous improvement where employees get better and better at handling difficult situations over time.

Emotions Are Contagious

For customer service employees, the job is even more challenging because emotions are contagious. Encounters with angry customers can leave employees feeling irritable, and that feeling can linger as they interact with other customers. Likewise, particularly outgoing customers can make employees feel upbeat and help them deliver a higher level of service to people they subsequently encounter.[6]

Looking back at that inglorious day when I hung up on a customer, I now understand how contagious emotions played a role in my actions. It seemed as if I was receiving anger from all sides. My boss was angry at me, my coworkers were annoyed with me, and my customers were furious. I was becoming angrier and angrier with each person I encountered. This anger reached its apex with the customer who wouldn't stop insulting me.

It may be tempting to observe situations like mine and think that customer service employees should simply resist getting infected with other people's emotions. Unfortunately, the contagious effects of other people's emotions are often experienced unconsciously. Employees might not even realize an upset customer is making them angry until the anger begins to impair their ability to provide good customer service.

In 2000, researchers at Uppsala University in Sweden published the results of an experiment that confirmed how people can unconsciously react to emotions expressed by others. Subjects in the experiment were exposed to images of people who were either smiling or looked angry. These images were flashed on a screen for just thirty milliseconds, which is too short a time for the conscious brain to notice the image, but long enough for the unconscious brain to process it. The happy or angry pictures were closely followed by an image of someone with a neutral expression that was displayed for five seconds. Throughout the experiment, subjects were connected to tiny electrodes that allowed the experimenters to measure the subjects' facial reactions.

The electrodes detected facial movements in the subjects that aligned with the pictures they were unconsciously exposed to. The group who saw images of people smiling displayed a higher level of activity in the muscles used to smile, while the group who saw pictures of angry people had a higher level of activity in the muscles that create a frown. None of the subjects was aware of seeing the happy or angry faces when debriefed after the experiment.[7]

You can have a little fun conducting your own version of this experiment by smiling at strangers in public. It works particularly well in a crowded area where many people are passing by, such as an airport or a shopping mall. Try to make eye contact and smile at people as they pass by and you'll be amazed at how many complete strangers automatically smile back.

Contagious negative emotions don't come exclusively from customers, bosses, and coworkers. Factors outside the work environment can influence employees' emotions. Personal problems, such as having an argument with a spouse, a sick child, or financial difficulties can all contribute to a sour mood. Something as simple as an inconsiderate driver encountered during an employee's morning commute can infect that employee's state of mind.

Companies that offer outstanding service strive to make their work environments as positive as possible. Positive emotions are just as contagious as negative feelings, and upbeat employees lead to happier customers and coworkers in a self-reinforcing cycle. These organizations foster an enjoyable work environment by helping employees create strong bonds with their coworkers, bosses, and the company as a whole.

Encouraging friendships among coworkers is an important first step. According to Tom Rath, a researcher at Gallup, employees with at least one coworker who is also a close friend are seven times more likely than other employees to be engaged in their jobs.[8] Friends make it easier for employees to keep their spirits high and to recover from negative situations.

Of course, friendships at work must form naturally, but companies can influence their development through a variety of strategies. Here are a few examples:

- Holding informal social events after work encourages employees to interact with one another in a casual setting.

- Varying work schedules and project assignments gives people the opportunity to work with a variety of coworkers.

- Hiring employees in groups or "cohorts" helps them become friendly with one another as they go through the shared experience of being new employees.

Bosses can also play a big role in helping employees maintain a positive frame of mind. A supportive supervisor helps employees recover quickly from encounters with difficult customers. On the other hand, an unfriendly boss generates negative emotions that tend to lead to poor service.

Supervisors need supervision, too. Executives need to be in tune with employees two or more levels below them so that they understand the impact supervisors are having on morale. Some organizations choose to augment direct observations with periodic 360-degree surveys in which managers are evaluated by their employees, or through workplace climate surveys where employee satisfaction is assessed along multiple dimensions, including their relationship with their direct supervisor.

This leads to the third level of responsibility: Senior executives need to make the company a place where employees want to work. It should be seen as a refuge, so even those employees experiencing personal problems can feel as though their burden is lifted when they come to work.

In 2010, 32 percent of companies on *Bloomberg Businessweek*'s annual list of the top-25 Customer Service Champs were also on *Fortune Magazine*'s list of the 100 Best Companies to Work For. Companies that make the Best Companies to Work For list have supportive leaders who inspire trust and a workplace where employee friendships are abundant. They tend to offer a better package of compensation, benefits, and other perks than their competitors because they understand the benefits of attracting top talent, having low turnover, and encouraging loyalty and productivity. Most important, employees have a sense of pride in their work and understand the value of their contributions to the company's success.[9]

The High Cost of Emotional Labor

Most customer service positions have standards governing the emotions that employees should express to their customers. These standards, called "display rules," include typical service behaviors such as making eye contact, smiling, and addressing people with a warm and friendly tone. They may be explicitly defined in a procedure or set of customer service standards, or implicitly expected as part of our cultural norms for customer service professionals.

Display rules are easy to follow when they're in sync with our genuine emotions. Smiling, making eye contact, and warmly addressing customers come naturally when we're in a good mood. However, these same rules can be exceedingly difficult to follow when our true emotions don't match. An employee who is experiencing anger, sadness, or frustration is still expected to smile at customers, but it's very hard to make that smile appear genuine.

Customers are usually able to perceive the difference between sincere expressions of emotion and employees who are engaged in what's called "surface acting," where the displayed emotion doesn't match the person's true feelings.[10] The airline industry is often cited as an example where people observe a stark contrast between the expected display rules and how flight attendants actually feel. Pacific Southwest Airlines (PSA) even played to this notion when it ran a funny ad campaign in 1979 called "Our Smiles Aren't Just Painted On." The commercials emphasized the authentic service of PSA flight attendants in contrast to competitors' disingenuous attempts to appear friendly.[11]

As a frequent traveler, I often have the chance to observe the gap between flight attendants' real and displayed feelings. I can overhear their candid conversations while riding on an airport shuttle bus or sitting near the galley on the airplane. Of all the airlines I've experienced, Southwest Airlines' flight attendants seem to be the happiest with their jobs, their coworkers, and their lives in general. This genuine happiness easily carries over to those moments when they are serving passengers. On the other hand, I've often observed flight attendants from other airlines complaining about their jobs, coworkers, or personal lives. This attitude clearly impacts their quality of service. This may be one more reason that Southwest Airlines consistently offers some of the best service in the airline industry.

The effort required to bridge the gap between the display rules and your actual emotions is known as "emotional labor." A little bit of emotional labor can be expected in any customer service role, but employees experiencing a large gap between their actual and displayed emotions over a prolonged period of time are highly susceptible to burnout. In much the same way that physical labor can tax our energy, exerting high amounts of emotional labor can leave people physically and mentally exhausted.[12] Employees experiencing burnout ultimately leave their jobs or—worse— continue in their positions long after they've stopped trying.

In 2005, the *Wall Street Journal* MarketWatch site surveyed a group of trade associations and human resources experts to compile a list of the ten occupations with the highest employee turnover. Not surprisingly, seven out of ten of these high-burnout jobs are in customer service. All of the positions require employees to regularly exert a high level of emotional labor.[13]

The costs of employee burnout and turnover are significant. There are direct costs that are fairly easy to calculate, such as the cost of recruiting, hiring, and training new employees to replace the ones who leave. Indirect costs, such as lost productivity and decreased revenue due to poor performance, are much harder to calculate precisely but are often far greater than the direct costs.

I once worked with a hospital to help reduce turnover among the staff of 200 nurses. The annual turnover rate was 30 percent, meaning the hospital had to hire an average of sixty nurses every year to replace those who left. The direct cost of hiring and training replacements was $300,000 per year. However, the hospital's chief financial officer estimated the indirect costs associated with turnover, including lost productivity, lower patient satisfaction, and decreased levels of patient care, were as high as $3,000,000 per year, or ten times as much as the direct costs. These indirect costs were hard to capture and measure, so an exact tally was elusive, but there was clearly a huge impact.

My work with this client focused on helping the hospital create a more positive and engaging environment. Management adjusted its hiring practices to find nurses who would be more likely to enjoy working there. It improved training programs to provide nurses with skills to effectively handle stressful situations. The hospital's managers learned how to provide more positive feedback and recognition to improve the work climate. Within eighteen months, these efforts paid off and the turnover rate was cut in half.

Emotional labor was another obstacle I faced when I hung up on that customer many years ago. My dislike for my job and my bosses was so strong that it was getting harder and harder to go to work each day. I started getting sick more often and found myself becoming increasingly irritable around my employees, my friends, and even my wife. As a customer service manager, I was expected to model all of the display rules you'd expect from a service employee, but my true emotions rarely matched those expectations.

Eventually, I felt burned out and began to look for a new job with a better work environment. As luck would have it, I quickly received two job offers. One position was as customer service manager for another call center; the other was as a customer service trainer for a parking management company. The call center job paid 20 percent more and was in an industry I was familiar with, but a quick tour of the work environment told me this company's culture wouldn't be much different from the one I was trying to escape from.

Despite the substantially lower salary, the customer service training position was more in line with my dream job. The person who would be my boss seemed wonderfully supportive and committed to creating an engaging work environment. In our interview, she spoke about her passion for the company and how the organization was truly committed to world-class customer service. The potential coworkers I met during the interview process were all intelligent, dedicated people who seemed like they'd be fun to work with.

Choosing the training job over the call center management role was one of the easiest career decisions I've ever made. I distinctly remember making the call to accept my new job while on jury duty. The emotional labor of my soon-to-be-former job was so taxing that jury duty was a pleasant respite. Who'd imagine that being out of the office for three days while serving on a jury would seem like a vacation?

There are two strategies that companies can use to help their employees avoid the painful effects of high levels of emotional labor. The first is to create a positive and supportive work climate, which has already been discussed in this chapter. The second strategy is to help employees in high-stress situations find ways to recover, much the same way you need to physically recover after a strenuous workout.

My favorite recovery technique is an "attitude anchor." An attitude anchor is something that secures your attitude in a positive place. For example, if I need help recovering from a stressful encounter with a customer, I might spend a few moments chatting with a trusted friend to lighten my mood and reset my attitude to a more positive frame of mind. Attitude anchors can also be used to maintain a healthy and positive outlook, such as regularly catching up with close friends regardless of whether I need their support in that moment.

Attitude anchors are inherently personal, so what works for one person may not work for someone else. Supervisors can help employees identify their own attitude anchors by having them make a list of "recovery" and "maintenance" anchors. I've listed mine in Figure 10-1.

Figure 10-1. Attitude anchors.

Recovery Anchors	Maintenance Anchors
• Talk to a trusted friend or coworker.	• Get regular exercise.
• Take a short walk and get some fresh air.	• Enjoy my morning coffee.
• Find a good joke or a cartoon.	• Listen to music.
• Take a deep breath and clear my mind.	• Relax while reading.
• Refocus on something positive.	• Spend time with friends and family.

Solution Summary: Helping Employees Overcome Emotional Roadblocks

Customer service is an emotional job. There are highs associated with knowing you helped someone, and there are lows that come from working with challenging customers, coworkers, or bosses. Helping employees avoid or manage negative emotions is essential to creating an organization that consistently serves its customers at the highest level.

Here is a summary of the solutions offered in this chapter:

- Make employees, not customers, the top priority for the organization. The employee-first approach fosters a supportive work environment, promotes a sense of belonging, and encourages self-esteem.

- Meet with employees—in a supportive and nonjudgmental way— after they have encountered an angry customer to help them learn from their experience and develop skills for handling similar situations in the future.

- Encourage employees to develop friendships with their coworkers, so they'll find more enjoyment in their work environment.

- Ensure that supervisors apply a positive and supportive leadership style that encourages dedication and commitment from employees.

- Make your company a place where employees can easily leave their personal troubles behind and look forward to coming to work each day.

- Help employees identify their personal attitude anchors to help them maintain a positive outlook or recover from a negative encounter.

Notes

1. A. H. Maslow, "A Theory of Human Motivation," *Psychological Review* 50 (1943), pp. 370–396.

2. Michael Sliter, Katherine Sliter, and Steve Jex, "The Employee as a Punching Bag: The Effect of Multiple Sources of Incivility on Employee Withdrawal Behavior and Sales Performance," *Journal of Organizational Behavior* 33, no. 1 (August 2011), pp. 121–139.

3. Adi Ignatius, "We Had to Own the Mistakes," HBR Interview with Howard Schultz, *Harvard Business Review,* July 2010.

4. Archives of *Fortune Magazine*'s annual "100 Best Companies to Work For" can be found at *CNNMoney.com* (http://money.cnn.com/magazines/fortune/best-companies/). Starbucks was ranked No. 24 in 2009, No. 93 in 2010, and No. 98 in 2011.

5. Archives of *Bloomberg Businessweek*'s annual "Customer Service Champs" list can be found on www.businessweek.com/archive/news.html. Starbucks was ranked No. 10 in 2007, No. 6 in 2008, and No. 13 in 2010.

6. Elaine Hatfield, John T. Cacioppo, and Richard L. Rapson, "Emotional Contagion," *Current Directions in Psychological Sciences* 2, no. 3 (June 1993), pp. 96–99.

7. Ulf Dimberg, Monika Thunberg, and Kurt Elmehed, "Unconscious Facial Reactions to Emotional Expressions," *Psychological Science* 11, no. 1 (January 2000), pp. 86–89.

8. Jennifer Robison, "What Are Workplace Buddies Worth?" *Gallup Management Journal,* October 12, 2006; http://gmj.gallup.com.

9. *Fortune* partners with the consulting firm Great Place to Work to compile its annual list. You can learn more about the criteria and selection process by visiting the website www.greatplacetowork.com/our-approach/what-is-a-great-workplace. There are also many "best places to work" awards sponsored by local chambers of commerce, business newspapers, or human resources associations. These awards typically have published criteria that you can use to benchmark your organization against proven best practices.

10. Alicia A. Grandey, "Emotion Regulation in the Workplace: A New Way to Conceptualize Emotional Labor," *Journal of Occupational Health Psychology* 5, no. 1 (2000), pp. 95–110.

11. You can view a number of PSA's ad campaigns on the online PSA history museum: www.jetpsa.com. One of the commercials is also easy to watch on YouTube: http://www.youtube.com/watch?v=OOtv1lQ3Sgw.

12. Grandey, "Emotion Regulation in the Workplace."

13. Kristen Gerencher, "Where the Revolving Door Is Swiftest: Job Turnover High for Fast-Food, Retail, Nursing, and Child Care," *MarketWatch.com,* February 23, 2005; www.marketwatch.com/story/job-turnover-highest-in-nursing-child-care-retail.

CHAPTER 11

Casualties of Cost Consciousness

*Seeing Customer Service as a Profit Generator
Rather Than a Cost Center*

A few years ago, I switched my home phone and Internet service to the local cable company because it promised faster web browsing and a lower price. The cable company's installer came to my house and got everything up and running in two hours.

However, a few days later I noticed that my house alarm wasn't working properly. Apparently, the cable company's installer hadn't reconnected the alarm to the new phone system, so my alarm couldn't connect to the alarm monitoring company. A second technician had to come spend another two hours finishing the installation.

Everything worked well for the next six months until a power outage knocked out my phone service. Even after power was restored I still couldn't get a dial tone, so I called the cable company's technical support hotline and spent thirty minutes on the phone working through the various remedies suggested by the phone representative. None of these attempts worked, so we scheduled a service call for a technician to come to my house.

The technician arrived within the promised four-hour window and went to work diagnosing the problem. He spent an hour and a half checking the phone system and even made several calls to his supervisor and other technicians to ask for help. The technician finally concluded that my loss of phone service was caused by a problem with my house alarm. He told me I'd need to call my alarm company to have someone from that company come out and fix it.

It took another series of phone calls and waiting through another four-hour service window for an alarm company technician to arrive. He spent two hours trying to find the problem until he decided the phone system was the culprit. The technician told me there was nothing he could do and the cable company needed to fix it. By now I'd been without home phone service for several days and was starting to wonder if it would ever be restored.

After another aggravating runaround with the cable company's technical support hotline and scheduling myself to be home for yet another four-hour window, a third cable technician arrived at my house. I could immediately tell this guy was different from the other technicians. He was a contractor rather than a cable company employee, and he seemed to have a lot more knowledge. It took him only a few minutes to figure out that my phone system had been configured incorrectly when it was originally installed, making it susceptible to failures like the one I was experiencing. He had everything corrected and my phone service restored inside of thirty minutes.

Counting the initial installation, it had taken four phone calls and four service appointments to install my home phone service. The cable company had tried to save money by assigning less experienced technicians to do the installation and initial repair, but this strategy backfired and cost the company substantially more than it should have. The company would have realized substantial cost savings and avoided a huge customer service issue if it had sent out a capable technician to install the system right the first time.

In this chapter, we'll see that executives, just like their employees, face obstacles to delivering outstanding service. We'll explore how customer service leaders often use incomplete data when deciding how to deliver the most cost-effective service. We'll also examine common blunders executives make that lead to higher costs and lower revenue over the long term.

Fuzzy Math

My experience with the cable company isn't unusual. A 2011 survey by ClickFox found that cable providers are the companies that customers find most frustrating to interact with.[1] There are famous examples of poor service from cable technicians, such as the viral video of a Comcast employee who fell asleep on a customer's couch after spending an hour on hold with his own office.[2]

Part of the reason customers receive such poor service is that many cable companies focus on cost control when designing their service delivery systems. To them, the cost of providing customer service and technical support is a necessary evil, not an opportunity to create a long-term relationship with their customers. In my case, I was victimized by a tiered support structure that assigns the least-expensive person possible to try to fix a problem before escalating the issue to a more skilled, and therefore more costly, technician.

In theory, this tiered approach saves money, but that idea is based on incomplete financial data. Cable company executives know how much they pay their telephone technical support reps, installers, repair technicians, and experienced contractors. What they don't always understand is how much they actually pay to make a complete installation.

Here's an estimate of the cost to install my phone system, using data from www.salary.com for reasonable estimates of average salaries for each position. For the sake of simplicity, this estimate doesn't include equipment, overhead, travel time, vehicle costs, or many other expenses that would substantially increase the actual final number.

Estimated Cost to Install My Internet System

$3.12 for the Inbound Sales representative, assuming 15 minutes	@ $12.50 per hour
$13.75 for the Technical Support representative, for 50 minutes	@ 16.50 per hour
$125.12 for the Installation and Repair technician (junior level), for 5.5 hours	@ $22.75 per hour
$16.00 for the Repair contractor (senior level), for 30 minutes	@ $32.00 per hour
$75.00 for the Billing credit issued for phone service outage	
$232.99 = Total estimated cost	

What would have happened if the cable company had simply sent a qualified installer to do the job right the first time? Let's assume that the senior-level contractor would need two hours to conduct the initial installation. At a rate of $32 per hour, plus the $3.12 paid to the inbound sales rep, the total cost of doing the installation right the first time would be $67.12. In other words, by cutting corners and assigning less expensive but unqualified employees to do the job, the cable company inflated its total installation cost by $165.87—or 247 percent.

Executives often find it hard to quantify the cost of poor service experiences like mine because the numbers are hidden in the financial reports they use to run their businesses. They can easily see how much revenue their company produced and how much their service technicians cost, but understanding the true cost of service is more elusive. It takes careful analysis to understand whether customer service processes are helping or hurting a company's profitability.

The chief financial officer of a now-defunct retailer once told me that he couldn't see the importance of fixing a glitch that mispriced items on the retailer's website and led to inaccurate inventory counts. To him, the expense of investing in new technology far outweighed the cost of a few errors. What he didn't understand was how those errors led to lost revenue and increased customer service costs, and ultimately caused customers to flee to the company's competitors. In the end, his company was doomed because he and his fellow executives didn't have a deeper understanding of their profit and loss statement and didn't see the financial value in identifying and fixing systemic customer service failures.

Some companies try to manage customer service by tracking various metrics, but these efforts will fail if the metrics aren't correlated to customer satisfaction. For instance, many call centers measure talk time—the average amount of time it takes to complete each phone call. The theory is that shorter phone calls are more economical since an employee can handle more calls per hour. More calls per hour means the company can hire fewer employees, lowering its effective cost per call.

Talk time is automatically tracked in most call centers, and supervisors can easily access this information and take action on it. Employees whose talk time is deemed too high can expect to hear from their supervisor and may even face disciplinary action. The inevitable result of emphasizing talk time is that employees focus on meeting a standard designed to control costs rather than solving customers' problems. This tends to increase call volume rather than reduce it. Total time on the phone, not the average time per call, is what really drives the cost of running a call center.

According to the call center research firm SQM Group, the average call center solves just 68 percent of customers' problems on the first call. That means that 32 percent of calls handled by the typical call center are wasteful. There's a far greater savings potential in reducing wasteful calls instead of just making each call shorter, but executives need to understand the causes of continued dissatisfaction and repeat calls before they can take action.[3]

Customer satisfaction, however, is a blind spot for many executives. A 2011 study published by the International Customer Management Institute found that only 67.8 percent of call centers surveyed capture any sort of customer satisfaction data.[4] I conducted my own informal study in January 2012 and found similar results across all industries. Executives look at financial statements and budgets to make business decisions, but they can't understand the impact of their decisions on customer service if the data isn't available.

There are many reasons executives don't insist on capturing and analyzing customer feedback. One CEO I know doesn't like the consumer ratings site Yelp because he believes people only write reviews to air grievances. Another CEO told me that he didn't feel a need to measure customer satisfaction because a few of his friends were saying good things, so he didn't think there were any problems. A third CEO told me that he wanted to track customer service, but a closer examination revealed he was only interested in converting more inquiries into sales and didn't truly believe that customer satisfaction had an impact on his business.

Companies that want to use outstanding service to drive profits must have a commitment from top executives. Because executive leaders rely on data to make decisions, that commitment must include capturing and analyzing customer satisfaction data. This data can take many forms, including customer satisfaction surveys, tracking repeat businesses, or monitoring what customers are saying about your company via social media and online ratings sites.

In 2004, the brokerage firm Charles Schwab was struggling, in large part because of poor client service. The company's founder and namesake took over the company after the board ousted David Pottruck as CEO, and Schwab made improving service a priority in his new role. One of his key actions was implementing a Net Promoter Score metric, which is created by surveying customers and asking them how likely they'd be to recommend the company to others. The survey categorizes customers as promoters, neutral, or detractors, and the Net Promoter Score is derived by subtracting the detractors from the promoters. This metric soon became as integral to decision making as the company's financial figures, and the Net Promoter Score was reviewed in executive committee meetings, shared on calls with stock analysts, and discussed in employee meetings.[5]

Focusing on both customer service and financial success helped Charles Schwab make a series of moves that might not have been made had the company focused on financials alone. The company cut prices and reduced or eliminated many fees so that it could offer its clients greater value. The company focused on building relationships with its clients rather than profiting solely from short-term transactions. In just two years, this strategy paid off and Charles Schwab's net profit rose from $286 million in 2004 to $1.2 billion in 2006.[6]

Less Is Often Less

It can be tempting for a business to try to increase profitability by reducing expenses. But businesses that focus on cutting costs without regard to customer satisfaction may inadvertently trigger a decline in revenue that far exceeds the benefits achieved by any cost savings.

I noticed an interesting sign one day while waiting for my sandwich at a convenience store deli. The large, handwritten sign was hanging above the self-serve coffee station:

NO FREE REFILLS!
(for any coffee)

NO EXCEPTIONS
(charged regular price for refills)

This unfriendly message was an attempt to control costs on two fronts. First, the store had installed a self-serve coffee station so that the busy cashier didn't have to take extra time to pour coffee for customers. Second, the store didn't want to give away coffee, because then the cashier would have to refill the coffee dispensers more often, which would take up the cashier's time and ultimately increase the store's costs.

The sign may have saved a few dollars on the store's annual coffee bill, but it also drove customers away. The sign told customers, "We're too busy to help you, and we don't think you deserve any extra coffee." Perhaps the store manager didn't realize customers could get a free cup of coffee at the local hardware store, the bank, the auto shop, or any number of other places that understood how the goodwill generated by offering free coffee far outweighs the small expense. Here at the convenience store, customers have already bought the first cup, so why begrudge them a free refill? Needless to say, I haven't been back.

Many retail department stores have cut back on labor expenses by reducing the number of associates on the sales floor. This move has undoubtedly yielded some savings, but the downside is that there are fewer employees helping customers make a selection or find the right size or suggesting additional items. In some cases, customers even have to hunt for a cashier just to ring up a purchase.

Restaurants suffer from the same challenge. Each fall, my Saturdays are typically spent at college football watch parties organized by local alumni clubs and held at various sports bars. A good server can keep a crowd happy—and add to the restaurant's bottom line—over the course of the four-hour game by periodically checking in to refill sodas and take another food or drink order. However, when restaurants cut back on staff, it's harder and harder for servers to provide prompt, personal attention for all their tables at these football watch parties. There have been many times when people in our group have decided against ordering an extra plate of nachos or one more beer because it took too long for our busy server to check on us.

Some companies have tried to reduce their reliance on costly employees by investing in self-service technology, but this strategy backfires if the technology isn't easy to use or becomes the source of customer frustration. Virtually all call centers rely on an automated phone menu as a way of routing customer calls and providing self-service options. This technology saves companies a few dollars by reducing the number of call center representatives needed, but it's also a near-universal source of customer aggravation.

Customers are frustrated with the endless arrays of options and automated voice-driven menus that never seem to work properly. When they finally do get someone on the phone, they're often asked to provide the same account number they were just required to punch in on the phone system. There are even websites such as GetHuman (www.gethuman.com) that offer tips and shortcuts for getting a live person on the phone.

Self-service kiosks have become increasingly prevalent in places such as grocery stores, airports, and parking facilities. In some instances, the speed and convenience offered by these self-service options have been a real benefit to customers. In other instances, they're an annoyance. An increasing number of grocers are now reducing or eliminating self-checkout stations as customer usage has declined. In 2011, supermarket chain Big Y announced it was completely phasing out self-checkout stations in its sixty-one stores after an internal study found the machines lengthened checkout times and decreased service quality as customers struggled to use the technology.[7]

Organizations committed to outstanding service avoid cutting costs for the sake of reducing expense alone. They understand the impact that cost-cutting measures will have on customer service, including the potential implications for lost revenue and efficiency. In some cases, the return on investment will be so difficult to calculate that leaders simply have to trust that doing the right thing for their customers will pay off in the long run.

I once delivered a customer service training class in a movie theater at a shopping mall. The participants were employees of the mall's parking garage, and the theater manager let us use the room at no cost. The manager even provided free popcorn and soft drinks for everyone to enjoy.

The class, which included a training video shown on the big screen, was a memorable experience for everyone.

At first glance, it might not seem like the theater manager had much to gain by waiving the theater rental fee, giving us free concessions, and paying employees to come in early to serve us. Sure, a better parking experience for theatergoers might generate a little extra revenue, but we were going to train our employees anyway. Yet this move paid off in the fantastic experience enjoyed by the fifty employees who attended the class. Those fifty employees were potential customers, along with their friends and family members who heard about the wonderful time they had at customer service training. The class was more than ten years ago, and I still frequent that theater even though it lacks modern stadium seating and is farther from home than other options.

Some investments do have a clear impact. When I shop at Bath and Body Works to buy a gift for my wife, I always feel out of my element until I'm inevitably approached by a helpful sales associate. The cheerful salespeople help me make selections that always end up pleasing my wife, and their expert suggestions frequently entice me to purchase more than I'd originally intended to buy. Bath and Body Works views its associates as people who generate revenue and promote repeat business, not as expenses to be minimized.

Self-service technology can also pay off if companies understand that the human element is still extremely important. I'm a huge fan of Mimeo. com, an on-demand printing company that lets you upload documents to a website, select the binding and finishing options you want, and then have a fantastically high-quality finished product delivered as early as the next morning. The website is easy to use, and there's always a customer service rep available if I need assistance.

Things have gone perfectly every time I've used Mimeo.com with just two exceptions. On one occasion, I uploaded a file in a format that didn't print very well, and the document was unusable. Thankfully, a helpful customer service rep walked me through the process of creating a better file and didn't charge me for the replacement order, even though it was my own error.

The second time something went wrong was when the delivery driver for a third-party shipping company accidentally delivered my order to the wrong address. It took some detective work to find out what happened since the delivery company's records indicated the order had been delivered to the correct address, but a Mimeo customer service rep eventually sent out a replacement order at no charge. In both instances, it was human error that caused the problem. It was also a human who quickly solved each problem I experienced with Mimeo, which is why I remain a loyal customer.

Problems can and will happen, but anything short of a swift resolution will infuriate customers and cause them to take their business elsewhere. In many cases, a friendly, well-trained person must be available to quickly assist a customer in need. A 2011 study commissioned by American Express found that 90 percent of U.S. customers wanted to speak to a real person over the phone to resolve their problems, while only 20 percent of customers found an automated phone menu acceptable.[8] It might be cheaper for Mimeo if it provided layers of phone menus and self-serve options to encourage me to resolve my problem without assistance from an expensive employee, but spending a little more on customer service allows Mimeo to earn my continued business even when I do encounter an occasional challenge.

Short-Term Gains That Spread Customer Ill Will

A number of years ago, I had to get the water pump replaced on my trusty Honda Accord. When I picked up the car from the repair shop, I noticed the final bill was several hundred dollars higher than the estimate. A closer look at the bill revealed that the mechanic had replaced my timing belt even though I didn't request it and it wasn't included in the estimate.

I asked to speak to the manager and showed him both my estimate and the repair bill. His initial response was to nonchalantly explain that they always replaced the timing belt when they replaced a water pump. He didn't know why this service wasn't included in the original estimate or why nobody from the shop had gotten my permission before adding such an expensive item, but he didn't seem to understand that it was a problem. The manager just shrugged and insisted that was normal procedure.

Replacing a timing belt is an expensive repair, and I had just had it done a few months earlier. If there was a problem with the belt, then the replacement should have been covered under warranty. If there wasn't anything wrong with the belt, then the manager was hoping I wouldn't put up too much of a fight when he tried to gouge me for a few hundred dollars.

I calmly asked the manager if there had been anything wrong with the timing belt the mechanic had replaced. He couldn't answer that question, so I gave him two options. He could either reinstall my old timing belt or give me the new one for free. He reluctantly decided to take the timing belt replacement off the bill.

This unethical attempt to pad their revenue cost the owners of this repair shop more than the price of the part and the mechanic's labor. My wife and I had both been taking our cars to this shop, but after this incident we vowed never to return. I imagine this type of business practice eventually caught up with them, because they are no longer in business.

The pursuit of revenue without regard to customer satisfaction led the video rental company Netflix to make not just one, but two colossal service blunders in 2011. It started when the company announced a 60 percent price increase on July 12, in an e-mail sent to subscribers and a post on the company blog. The backlash from surprised and outraged customers generated a wave of negative press for the company and prompted many people to cancel their service.[9]

Customers were still fuming about the price hike when Netflix made its second blunder. On September 18, Netflix CEO Reed Hastings announced on the Netflix blog that the company was separating its online video streaming and DVD rental services into two separate businesses.

This move would require customers to maintain two separate accounts to manage and pay for their online and DVD video rentals separately. Hastings explained the move was necessary because the two services had different cost structures and marketing challenges. He also offered an apology for the way Netflix communicated the price increase it announced earlier in the year but defended the move as a necessary business decision.[10]

This time, consumer outrage was so deafening that Netflix reversed its plans to separate video streaming and DVD rentals into separate businesses. However, the damage had already been done. Netflix lost 800,000 subscribers and its stock declined 75 percent in the third quarter of 2011. The company also suffered a 14 percent decrease in customer satisfaction on the 2011 American Customer Satisfaction Index, one of the most dramatic one-year declines ever recorded.[11]

I was one of those Netflix subscribers affected by the 60 percent price increase. Like many customers, I considered canceling my service and tried to find a reasonable alternative. My surprising conclusion was that even after the price increase, Netflix still offered the best deal for the services I used. The rate hike was the product of sound financial and marketplace analysis, but the company unnecessarily alienated customers because it didn't consider the strong emotional reaction such a large price increase would generate. As a result of my analysis, I remained a Netflix member, but I stopped referring the service or giving gift subscriptions as I had in the past.

Some companies have resorted to new fees as a way of raising revenue without increasing advertised prices. Airlines have been steadily implementing fees for many accommodations that used to be free, such as checked bags, seat assignments, and in-flight snacks. Event ticketing companies charge convenience fees, transaction fees, and ticket delivery fees on top of the ticket prices. Hotels assess Internet fees, resort fees, and charge for bottled water in addition to the room rate. The list goes on and on.

These fees can provide much-needed revenue, especially in industries that consistently struggle to be profitable. However, they can also alienate customers. In December 2011, Verizon Wireless announced it was instituting a $2 fee for customers who made certain payments online or via telephone. The resulting anger from customers already upset at fees from other companies was so overpowering that Verizon quickly backtracked and scrapped the fee one day later.[12]

While executives face pressure from shareholders to find innovative ways to grow revenue, smart companies recognize that outstanding customer service can lead to better results in the long run. Customer service leaders should evaluate any plan to raise prices or implement new fees against the potential impact on customer retention, revenue per customer, and referrals. Failure to consider the full impact can result in customer defections and lost sales.

Verizon Wireless provides a great case study on the value of customer retention. When the company announced that $2 fee, its basic rate plan was $39.99 per month, which is $959.76 over the life of a standard two-year contract—and that doesn't include the price of a phone, accessories, data plans for smartphones, or more expensive plans that could drive the revenue from a single customer even higher. In retrospect, it seems pretty silly to risk a customer relationship worth at least $959.76 over a $2 fee.

Resisting the temptation to raise prices or increase fees can also lead to more revenue. One of my favorite restaurants in San Diego, Terra American Bistro, lowered its prices when the establishment moved to a new location. The restaurant had terrific food and service to begin with, so the new prices caused my wife and me to go there more often. The lower prices meant we spent a little less money per visit, but we went there twice as often in the first year at the new location than we had during the previous year. Many other customers obviously felt the same way, because the new location has consistently been much busier than the old one.

Referrals are free advertising for your business. Companies that provide great value by keeping prices reasonable and delivering outstanding service are much more likely to have their customers refer new customers. On the other hand, negative publicity, such as Netflix experienced in reaction to its price increase, can drive potential customers away.

In 2004, I was elected to serve a two-year term as membership director for the San Diego chapter of the American Society for Training and Development (ASTD), a professional association for corporate trainers. During my two-year term we increased chapter membership by 67 percent without any advertising or special promotions. Instead, our leadership team relied on referrals to help the organization grow. We worked diligently to engage members on a personal level, find out their interests, and provide valuable services in return for their membership dues, so members would encourage their colleagues to join the chapter, too.

Solution Summary: Positioning Customer Service as a Profit Generator

It can be difficult for executives to consider the impact on customer service when making strategic decisions about their companies. They often lack direct contact with customers, and the limited customer service data they have is not as comprehensive, easy to understand, or reliable as the financial reports they're so comfortable using. However, leaders must understand that outstanding customer service isn't a cost to be minimized; it's an investment in future profitability.

Here is a summary of the solutions discussed in this chapter:

- Executives must capture and analyze customer satisfaction data to ensure strategic decisions are not based solely on financial metrics.

- Customer service leaders should dig deeper into their financial statements to understand the true cost of poor customer service.

- The long-term benefit of customer service investments should be carefully understood before implementing cost-cutting measures that might drive customers away.

- Investing in the right number of qualified, well-trained employees pays off when the employees are able to drive sales and customer satisfaction.

- Self-service technology can be tempting because of the promised cost savings, but the expense of lost customers and lost revenue can be high if the technology doesn't function properly or customers find it irritating or difficult to use.

- Executives should carefully consider the impact of any price or fee increase on customer retention, revenue per customer, and referrals before making a final decision.

Notes

1. "Customer Tipping Point Survey Results: How Much Is Poor Customer Service Costing Your Business?" ClickFox, Inc., 2011.

2. You can view the hilarious video of a sleeping Comcast repair technician on YouTube: www.youtube.com/watch?v=CvVp7b5gzqU.

3. Mike Desmarais, "First Call Resolution (FCR)—The Metric That Matters Most," SQM Group, http://www.sqmgroup.com/fcr-metric-that-matters-most.

4. International Customer Management Institute, "2011 Research Report: Balancing Call Center Efficiency and the Customer Experience" (Colorado Springs: ICMI, 2011).

5. Fred Reichheld and Rob Markey, *The Ultimate Question 2.0: How Net Promoter Companies Thrive in a Customer-Driven World* (Boston: Harvard Business School Publishing, 2011).

6. Ilana DeBare, "Interview with CEO of the Year Charles Schwab," *San Francisco Chronicle*, April 9, 2007.

7. Heather Malcolm, "Human Touch Trumps Self-Service for Mass. Supermarket Chain," *USA Today*, September 16, 2011.

8. Echo Research, "2011 Global Customer Service Barometer: Market Comparison of Findings," research report commissioned by American Express; available at http://about.americanexpress.com/news/docs/2011x/AXP_2011_csbar_market.pdf.

9. Jessie Becker, "Netflix Introduces New Plans and Announces Price Changes," Netflix U.S. & Canada Blog, July 12, 2011.

10. Reed Hastings, "An Explanation and Some Reflections," Netflix U.S. & Canada Blog, September 18, 2011.

11. Claes Fornell, "ACSI Commentary February 2012," The American Customer Satisfaction Index, February 21, 2012.

12. Ron Lieber, "After Outcry, Verizon Abandons $2 Fee," *New York Times*, December 30, 2011.

PART III

Putting Lessons into Action

CHAPTER 12

Getting Started

One of my favorite training exercises to use with customer service leaders is called the Road Trip Activity. I tell them that they have one minute to brainstorm items they'd take with them on a road trip, and I encourage them to work with the people sitting near them. "Is everyone ready?" I ask before starting the timer. They're always eager to get started.

The participants aren't given any rules other than my request to brainstorm, but their behavior is remarkably consistent every time I run this activity. People quickly form small groups and excitedly share ideas. Most people begin with the assumption that the activity is a competition and the team that brainstorms the most items will win. One person in each group inevitably takes charge of writing down everyone's ideas.

About thirty seconds into the exercise, it dawns on one or two people that nobody asked a very important question. Gradually a few others realize it, too. However, most people complete the activity without noticing they're missing the most important piece of information.

Where are we going?

After the minute is up, I ask the various groups to share how many items they came up with. Even then, there are still some groups that haven't caught on as they excitedly share their totals and look around the room to see if they brainstormed the most items. Finally, someone in the class asks the most important question out loud: "Where are we going?" You can almost see the lightbulbs go on over everyone's head.

I run the activity a second time, but now I give them a specific destination, such as a theme park, a baseball game, or the beach a few hours' drive from where the class is being held. Several items on the second list carry over from the first, but there are also new items essential to enjoying the destination, such as bringing a bathing suit and a towel to a day at the beach. The second list is almost always much shorter than the first.

This activity demonstrates how easy it is to engage in action without having a clear objective. When we're extremely busy it may seem like we're getting something done, even when we're heading in the wrong direction or just spinning around in circles. We can avoid this trap only when we know where we're headed before we start our journey. Only then can we make the preparations that will ensure we get where we want to be.

In this final chapter, we'll focus on practical ways to implement the ideas and advice described in previous chapters. We'll start by exploring some of the pitfalls that can cause a customer service initiative to fail. Next, we'll look at three steps organizations can take to overcome the obstacles outlined in this book and achieve consistently positive results. Finally, I'll offer one last reminder that outstanding customer service employees may already be working for your company. All you need to do is help them be great!

What to Know Before You Get Started

It's important to know why customer service initiatives fail before you get started on the journey to improve service in your own organization. This knowledge will at once help you avoid those mistakes and chart a course toward success.

The first cause of failure is what I call "Harvard Business Review management." That's when leaders read about the latest management trend in *Harvard Business Review* or another top-notch management publication and decide to implement the idea in their own organization, without fully understanding the concept or what's required to make it succeed. The inevitable result of this approach is the leader severely underestimating the commitment and resources necessary to obtain the same results described in the magazine article or business book.

As a national account manager for a company selling uniforms, it was my job to work with my assigned clients to keep them happy and grow the business. One day, the general manager of our group announced his decision to reorganize all the account managers and support staff into self-directed teams. The general manager felt this approach would allow us to improve client service and increase sales by working in small teams focused on specific industries.

The unintended result of his decision was inefficiency, declining sales, and low morale—exactly the opposite of what he'd anticipated. People who were used to working independently, even to the point of competing with coworkers for territory and sales leads, were now expected to collaborate but were given no training on how to do so. The reorganization also angered many customers who were upset at suddenly being assigned a new account manager. Within six months, the business unit's performance was so bad that the company began laying off people or transferring them to other departments. A year later, the entire group was gone.

The concept of self-directed work teams was a hot management trend when our general manager made his decision. It was the subject of countless magazine articles and case studies that profiled companies implementing this concept with great success. In the end, the initiative failed because the general manager announced the strategy but did little to ensure it was implemented successfully.

This general manager is not alone in his actions. Many executives pass around an interesting article to their teams with a handwritten note exclaiming "Let's do this!" Some leaders distribute books to their managers as part of an ad-hoc leadership book club. (Is that how you came to read this book?)

The problem with this approach is that it's just the beginning of the journey rather than the end. Simply announcing "Teams!" doesn't mean everyone will suddenly begin working in well-coordinated groups to the immense delight of their customers. Proclaiming "Customers are our number-one priority!" won't change a thing until things are actually changed.

Another way for a customer service initiative to fail is to make it a project that people work on temporarily or in their spare time. This arrangement implies that customer service is an afterthought rather than a real priority. It makes it easy for the initiative to be set aside when operational issues arise or the management team gets distracted by the next management fad.

Outstanding customer service needs to be hardwired into the way your company does business if you want your organization's service to consistently reach that level. It should be factored into strategic decisions, as we discussed in Chapter 11. It must be ingrained in the culture that was described in Chapter 6, and considered when developing policies and procedures, as we covered in Chapter 5. In my experience as a customer service consultant, this is the clear difference between companies whose initiatives succeed and those whose initiatives fail.

Yet one more way for a customer service initiative to fail is when it starts with training, since the training is being implemented before critical decisions are made. In their book *Courageous Training,* employee performance experts Robert Brinkerhoff and Tom Mooney state that companies must first set clear goals, identify the actions employees need to take to achieve those goals, and only then determine what training is needed to help employees achieve the desired performance. Companies that launch training programs without setting goals or clearly defining desired employee behaviors don't really know what training needs to be offered or why it's important.

I often respond to training requests from my clients by asking, "How will we know if this training program is successful?" The question sparks an important conversation when my clients haven't thought through how training connects to business results. This discussion usually results in a much smaller and more focused training plan. And, much like the Road

Trip Activity, the plan often includes elements that wouldn't have been incorporated if we had started training without verifying the objectives first.

The First Three Steps in the Journey to Outstanding Service

Every journey begins with the first step. In this case, I'll offer you the first three—with the caveat that they're easy to understand in concept but can be difficult to implement and master: 1) Clearly define outstanding service, 2) use this definition as a compass to guide everything you do, and 3) reinforce constantly.

Step 1: Clearly Define Outstanding Service

What does outstanding service mean to your organization or your department? We covered the hallmarks of a clear definition in Chapter 6 when we discussed the importance of creating a customer-focused culture. These three characteristics bear repeating here:

1. The definition is simple and easily understood.

2. It describes the type of service we want to achieve for our customers.

3. It reflects both who we are now and who we aspire to be in the future.

Here are a few examples, taken from some of the success stories described earlier in the book:

- *Southwest Airlines.* The mission of Southwest Airlines is dedication to the highest quality of Customer Service delivered with a sense of warmth, friendliness, individual pride, and Company Spirit.

- *True Value.* Our vision: to help every True Value be the best hardware store in town.

- *L.L.Bean.* Sell good merchandise at a reasonable profit, treat your customers like human beings, and they will always come back for more.

- *REI.* REI's passion for the outdoors runs deep. Our core purpose is to inspire, educate, and outfit people for a lifetime of outdoor adventure and stewardship.

- *Starbucks.* Our mission: to inspire and nurture the human spirit— one person, one cup, and one neighborhood at a time.

Outstanding service can be defined by a mission statement, a vision, a set of company values, a motto, a slogan, a credo, or anything else that's important to the organization and its employees. There's no one right way to do it. All that matters is that outstanding service is clearly defined and that the definition is infused into everything the company does.

Step 2: Use This Definition as a Compass to Guide Everything You Do

Your definition of outstanding customer service should be considered whenever a decision is made that has an impact on customer service. Chapters 2 through 11 each outline a specific obstacle that employees, teams, or organizations may face. Below are ten questions to help you assess, chapter by chapter, whether you're heading in the right direction or if you need to adjust your course. For each "No" answer, I recommend that you revisit that chapter and identify the actions necessary to get back on track.

1. Do we make it easy for our customers to be right? (Chapter 2)

2. Do our employees love to provide the level of service they're asked to give their customers? (Chapter 3)

3. Are employees able to serve their customers without feeling caught between what the company wants them to do and what the customer desires? (Chapter 4)

4. Do our policies, procedures, and work flows make it easy for our employees to delight our customers? (Chapter 5)

5. Do we have a strong, customer-focused culture? (Chapter 6)

6. Are employees able to focus their attention on providing the highest level of customer service? (Chapter 7)

7. Do employees clearly understand that customer service is their top priority? (Chapter 8)

8. Are employees given the tools and guidance necessary to help them empathize with their customers? (Chapter 9)

9. Does our workplace actively encourage positive feelings and emotions? (Chapter 10)

10. Do our leaders use customer service metrics as a guide when making strategic decisions? (Chapter 11)

Step 3: Reinforce Constantly

The third step in the journey is a never-ending process of constantly reinforcing customer service expectations with employees. Employees understand the importance of an activity or a cultural value by how it's emphasized. I once knew a manager whose sole action to help employees improve their level of service was a tersely worded memo attached to their paychecks. He never provided training, coaching, or reinforcement of any kind, so it should have been no surprise that performance never improved. Despite the manager's strongly worded memo, his actions suggested that customer service really wasn't that important.

Leaders who make customer service a priority take every opportunity to reinforce the message with their employees. Here are just a few examples illustrating how this message reinforcement can be done:

- Hold regular meetings to discuss customer service with employees.

- Post visual customer service reminders, such as illustrative posters on bulletin boards.

- Frequently provide employees with individual feedback.

- Give employees regular updates on their progress toward meeting customer service goals.

- Deliver periodic refresher courses to reinforce customer service skills.

- Organize committees to tackle specific customer service challenges.

- Pick a new customer service skill to focus on each week as a way to provide ongoing reminders and maintain constant awareness. (You can sign up for a free Customer Service Tip of the Week at www. toistersolutions.com/ideas.)

A Final Note: Your Worst Employee Might Be Your Best

I'll never forget my first assignment as a training supervisor at a catalog company. On my first day on the job I was asked to investigate problems with one of my night shift trainers, whom we'll call Nicole (not her real name). I was given two weeks to report back to my boss with either a decision to fire Nicole or a plan to improve her performance.

It was clear that my boss thought Nicole would need to be fired. She was concerned that Nicole was insubordinate and a divisive influence on the team. She'd heard complaints that Nicole refused to use some of the training materials that all our trainers were required to use. Some of the other trainers had complained that Nicole wasn't a team player, and my boss had made similar observations herself.

My team was responsible for training the customer service representatives who worked in two of the company's call centers, which were about ten miles apart. Most of the department, including my boss, worked in the larger of the two facilities, but Nicole worked in the smaller call center. The night shift ran from 4:00 p.m. to midnight, so she had infrequent contact with my boss and with the department's other trainers.

The natural starting point for my assignment was to spend some time with Nicole so that I could make an assessment based on my own observations. Nicole was a single mother who worked the night shift in order to care for her daughter during the day and have her mother watch her daughter while she went to work at night. As a young supervisor, I was nervous about making a decision that would have such a big impact on someone's livelihood. At the same time, I wanted to be good at my job and please my boss, and I knew my boss expected me to be able to make tough decisions.

It didn't take much time with Nicole to identify the major obstacles that hindered her performance. One obstacle was the training material Nicole was expected to use. She didn't deny that there were some materials she refused to use in her training classes, but she explained that those materials didn't reflect the call center's current policies. Nicole had repeatedly asked for updated materials from the employee responsible for maintaining the training materials in all our call centers, but Nicole was told that the documentation specialist was three months behind on her work and couldn't make the requested changes anytime soon.

This left Nicole with the choice to either use outdated materials in her classes or make adjustments on her own, so she could train new hires on current policies. She knew the call center supervisors her trainees would report to after training expected their employees to be fully trained, so her credibility would be questioned if she used the old materials. Her decision to make her own materials came from a refusal to let the documentation specialist's backlog be an excuse for not properly training new employees. Interestingly, it was the documentation specialist who had been complaining to my boss about Nicole's refusal to use the old materials.

Another obstacle was Nicole's schedule. Our department had a team meeting at the larger call center every Thursday, and all the trainers were expected to attend. The meeting started at 4:00 p.m., when the second shift arrived, and typically lasted until 5:00 p.m. Nicole's classes ran from 6:00 p.m. to midnight. It was a thirty-minute drive between call centers at that time of day, so that left her only a half hour to prepare for the evening's class. This schedule understandably put her in a rush to leave the weekly meeting, but her coworkers mistook her anxiousness as an unwillingness to create personal connections with the rest of the team.

After a short investigation, I went back to my boss and delivered a surprising report. Nicole shouldn't be fired. In fact, she was one of our best trainers!

Fixing the negative perceptions about Nicole's performance took some time, but the solutions were simple. The documentation specialist reported to my boss, so my boss directed her to reprioritize her work to make the necessary updates to the training materials. I allowed Nicole to attend the weekly meeting via conference call, so she'd have enough time to prepare for that evening's training class. I also adjusted Nicole's schedule so that she occasionally had a few days when she wasn't training and could create stronger relationships with her colleagues by working with them on special projects.

This experience stayed with me because it started with the assumption that Nicole was a rogue employee with a bad attitude who needed to be fired. Yet it turned out that she was someone who cared deeply about doing a great job. She just needed help to remove the obstacles that stood in her way. Nicole flourished once the path to success was cleared. In fact, she was promoted into my boss's job just five years later.

There are countless employees like Nicole whose hidden potential is just waiting to be uncovered. It's hard to assess the capabilities of these employees when significant obstacles remain in place, and the challenges they face are sometimes so severe that poor service is the inevitable result. Of course, there are a few people who aren't able to improve under any circumstances, but the vast majority of customer service employees can do great things when given the opportunity.

I believe the fundamental mission for every customer service leader is to help employees serve customers at the highest level. You start by identifying and removing the obstacles that stand in your employees' way. It takes patience and understanding, because even the best of us sometimes falter.

Above all else, customer service leaders must remember that while customer service can be difficult, their job is to make great performance easy.

Index